S0-ASD-788

Taking Your
Course Online

An Interdisciplinary Journey

Taking Your Course Online

An Interdisciplinary Journey

edited by

Kathleen M. Torrens
University of Rhode Island

José A. Amador
University of Rhode Island

INFORMATION AGE PUBLISHING, INC.
Charlotte, NC • www.infoagepub.com

Library of Congress Cataloging-in-Publication Data

Taking your course online : an interdisciplinary journey / edited by
Kathleen M. Torrens, Josi A. Amador.
    p. cm.
Includes bibliographical references.
ISBN 978-1-61735-593-6 (pbk.) – ISBN 978-1-61735-594-3 (hardcover) –
ISBN 978-1-61735-595-0 (ebook)
1. Education, Higher–Computer-assisted instruction. I. Torrens, Kathleen
M. II. Amador, Josi A.
LB2395.7.T35 2011
378.1'7344678–dc23

                                                          2011031945

Copyright © 2012 Information Age Publishing Inc.

All rights reserved. No part of this publication may be reproduced, stored in a
retrieval system, or transmitted, in any form or by any means, electronic, mechanical,
photocopying, microfilming, recording or otherwise, without written permission
from the publisher.

Printed in the United States of America

DEDICATION

This book would not have been possible for me to contribute to, much less help to orchestrate, without the early inspiration I received from Jeannette E. Riley. She introduced me to online teaching and learning, patiently waiting through my doubt, ineptitude, and resistance to that glorious "See? I told you!" moment. I am also grateful for all the opportunities I have had to learn, hone my skills, and work with faculty and students in this important and life-changing educational endeavor. Finally, I offer grateful thanks to my co-editor, José Amador, who came up with the brilliant idea for this collection.

—Kathleen Torrens
University of Rhode Island

To my students, who've been willing to go on the online journey with me; to my fellow online teachers, for their willingness to share their triumphs and tribulations; to my co-editor, Kathleen Torrens, for her willingness to jump head-first into this project; to my family—for being generous with my time.

—José Amador
University of Rhode Island

CONTENTS

SECTION I

HUMANITIES

SECTION II
SCIENCE AND MATHEMATICS

SECTION III
THE PROFESSIONS

CONCLUSIONS

PREFACE

Our book focuses on online pedagogy and the challenges and opportunities incumbent in the transformation of a face-to-face college course. It is intended as a resource and support for new online teachers—a source of ideas and strategies from a variety of disciplinary perspectives as well as pedagogical perspectives—and for those experienced in the online environment. The book meets the needs of faculty new to online teaching by providing them a wide variety of perspectives—pedagogical, multidisciplinary, class size and level—by faculty with varying degrees of previous experience who have recently made the transition from face-to-face to online. Their advice and recollections offer a fresh, contemporary perspective on the subject. For administrators and faculty experienced with online instruction, the collection works as a resource for ideas intended to sustain the vibrancy and efficacy of the online environment.

Practitioners using this book will learn how to turn their face-to-face course into an online course successfully, understand best practices for transitioning courses/online teaching, minimize errors and avoid pitfalls in the transition process, and maximize learning. Faculty development professionals can use this book as a resource to teach faculty from a wide range of disciplines how to transition from the actual to the virtual classroom. Administrators—such as deans and program chairs—will gain useful insights into ways to think about taking entire programs online, as well as how to guide faculty in their development of pedagogical skills pertinent to online learning.

The book includes the experiences of a cohort of faculty that responded to a university-wide call for faculty interested in developing online courses for the summer session. These faculty participated in a series of eight work-

Taking Your Course Online: An Interdisciplinary Journey, pages ix–x
Copyright © 2012 by Information Age Publishing
All rights of reproduction in any form reserved.

shops during the Spring 2009 semester that addressed various aspects of developing online courses and online pedagogy. All of the authors taught their new online course over a 10-week summer session in 2009, and many of them have done so subsequently as well. Their experiences have great currency in the ever-changing world of online teaching. Because the collection represents the work of teachers exposed to best practices and many discussions concerning rigor, assessment, and accountability, it provides support for the viability of online teaching/learning in an environment frequently plagued by doubts about its effectiveness. A key concern of those faculty and administrators charged with the development of online programming surrounds ways to ensure academic integrity, vitality, and challenge. Our entries deal, in varying ways, specifically with those concerns.

FOREWORD

Taking Your Course Online: An Interdisciplinary Approach will be a useful resource for college faculty teaching online for the first time as well as for those experienced in online teaching. A major strength in the book is that it is written *by* faculty *for* faculty, and that feature plays out in several important ways.

For starters, the book focuses on questions and challenges faculty encounter in trying to transform face-to-face courses to online offerings rather than focusing on the latest technology and the wonderful things it can do. When faculty see a pedagogical need, many want to learn about cutting-edge technology applications, but that is not where most start.

Most faculty start the transformation process by wondering how they will present content, how they will engage students in exploring and applying that content, and how they will assess learning in their online courses. They quickly discover that merely assigning reading, posting PowerPoint notes from their lectures in face-to-face classes, providing questions for online discussions, and giving periodic quizzes or exams do not work for all or even most students. To succeed, many of today's students need more structure, more prompting, and more feedback on their learning efforts; this seems especially so in online courses

We know that many college students have underdeveloped skills in learning from reading. Their assumptions about how much time they need to spend studying differ pretty dramatically from faculty expectations. Many are unaccustomed to learning independently; they expect faculty to tell them what exactly they need to know, to spell out what they need to do, and to proceed in incremental steps. Differences between student and fac-

Taking Your Course Online: An Interdisciplinary Journey, pages xi–xii
Copyright © 2012 by Information Age Publishing
All rights of reproduction in any form reserved.

ulty expectations become even more exaggerated when students taking on-line courses assume these courses will be less demanding than face-to-face courses, a challenge which some of these chapter authors address.

There are no easy solutions to these challenges, but this book is packed with suggestions on how to address them. Chapter authors write candidly about things they tried, what worked and what did not, and provide ideas on what they plan to try next.

The interdisciplinary nature of this book is also worth noting. In discussing their attempts to transform their face-to-face courses to online courses, chapter authors identify many common questions, issues, and problems. Faculty are often surprised to discover that colleagues in different disciplines both confront similar challenges and have transferable ideas about how to address them. This is a book that could foster interdisciplinary dialogue about a host of pedagogical issues.

Finally, editors Kathleen Torrens and José Amador have done an excellent job in outlining and holding chapter authors to an organizational framework that maintains focus. Each chapter begins with a description of the content and context for the course being taken online. Authors then identify the main issues they experienced in transforming their courses. Finally, they discuss and reflect upon policies, activities, and assignments that they developed to address those issues.

Whether you are just thinking about taking your course online or are already an experienced online instructor, you will find the diverse teaching narratives in this book helpful in the development of your online pedagogy.

Dr. Bette LaSere Erickson
Director, Instructional Development Program
University of Rhode Island

ACKNOWLEDGEMENTS

We must acknowledge the generous contributions of time and support that the Online Faculty Fellows Program received from the University of Rhode Island's Office of the Provost, the URI Instructional Development Program, the cadre of workshop leaders, and the workshop participants. The program made possible opportunities for networking and learning, as well as a productive space of engagement with new technologies, pedagogies, and ideas. The results of the workshops, both positive and less so, provide useful information for present and future educators interested in the online environment.

Taking Your Course Online: An Interdisciplinary Journey, page xiii
Copyright © 2012 by Information Age Publishing
All rights of reproduction in any form reserved.

CHAPTER 1

INTRODUCTION

Kathleen M. Torrens

Online learning is the modern version of distance education, whose roots extend at least to the 19th century, when learning by correspondence began to take shape. The first official recognition of higher education by correspondence—or distance—came in 1883 by Chautauqua College of Liberal Arts, according to Bizhan Nasseh (1997), in his essay "A Brief History of Distance Education." From correspondence programs, to distance education programs featuring televised broadcasts of lectures, to real-time distance learning, to web-based online education, the trajectory leading to today's online learning decries the predictions made that it would never take the place of, be as effective as, or mean as much as, the face-to-face classroom featuring the flesh-and-blood professor and student.

The current educational and economic moment sees colleges, universities, and corporations leaping onto the online learning bandwagon. Recognizing the value-added elements of using technology to deliver content, engage students and clients, ameliorate challenges of distance and time commitments, and maximize space usage, these institutions have embarked on a path fraught with challenges as well as opportunities. In its early stages, online education was considered a matter of simply taking information from its hard-copy or face-to-face format and putting it into a technology-enhanced format, a straightforward matter of conversion. Now, however,

Taking Your Course Online: An Interdisciplinary Journey, pages 1–3
Copyright © 2012 by Information Age Publishing
All rights of reproduction in any form reserved.

1

after more than two decades of study, development and refinement by practitioners and students, online pedagogy is a recognized process and methodology which is not as easy as it might look. Transforming a bricks-and-mortar class for the online environment requires careful reflection on a plethora of issues that range from access to—and comfort level with—technology (for both teacher and student), to student preparation, to learning outcomes and evaluation.

This book features the voices of educators who accepted the challenge to transform one of their face-to-face courses to online. They participated in a semester-long "Online Fellows" pilot program at the University of Rhode Island that covered best practices of syllabus construction, online course design, student engagement and assessment, and considerations of academic integrity. Each participant was charged with delivering an online course in the ensuing summer session. The task of transforming a face-to-face course to online was accomplished concurrent with the program's workshops. The program allowed for face-to-face mentoring, group discussions, and a forum to deal with frustrations, some of which related to the transformation process and others that emerged from changes in the online learning management systems used by the institution. The progress of each participant's course construction was showcased during a culminating "show and tell" session at the end of the semester. Participants represented a broad spectrum of academic homes, from landscape architecture to math to criminal justice to nursing. Further, they were transforming courses across varying levels of depth and rigor, ranging from introductory nursing to upper-level communication and media classes.

As noted above, the workshop ended with a "show and tell" where participants demonstrated their progress on the online courses. That these courses modeled best practices in a wide variety of disciplines indicates, at least anecdotally, the success of the training program. Nevertheless, as evidenced by the essays included in this collection, not every first time "onliner" had a great experience, nor are all of them ready to try again right away, but it seems safe to say that they all learned something valuable, whether about teaching and learning, the online environment, or about themselves as educators and people.

Based on the results of the pilot workshop program, the University of Rhode Island has moved forward with some institutionalization of their online offerings, with an eye toward developing a centralized unit overseeing issues of teaching, learning, and assessment that will include a sizeable component of online courses. As millions of students worldwide enroll in online courses, the need for institutions of higher learning to meet the challenge of providing high quality programs is clear. And, as articulated by a 2006 research study by Kim and Bonk in *Educause Quarterly*, the needs for pedagogically competent faculty, well-supported technology, and students prepared to self-regulate and to engage with technology are paramount... and complex. Addressing the multiple challenges of providing quality online instruction, whether in a strictly online format or a blended or hybrid form, requires heavy institutional commitment at all levels. The workshops from which this book emerged provide one example of a means to investigate those challenges and to begin the framing of a set of strategies for moving forward.

ORGANIZATION OF THE BOOK

The book is organized into three sections by academic area. The three sections are Humanities, Science and Math, and The Professions. Contributors shared common concerns across disciplines and pedagogical motives, ranging from motivating students to the entire issue of transforming the bricks-and-mortar class to the online environment. The stories are not all success stories, so readers may avoid some of the pitfalls encountered by our contributors.

Each essay begins with a brief abstract of the content and includes the academic context of the course, the main issues experienced with the transformation, and concluding comments intended to be helpful to the reader, regardless of the reader's academic position. For example, readers will encounter the pedagogical challenges faced by each writer, from creating immediacy to engaging students in problem-based learning to facilitating student discussions online. Each participant worked hard to create a learning environment in her or his course that would enable the achievement of specific objectives. What emerges from the collection as a whole is a multidisciplinary snapshot of transformative pedagogy, by practitioners working to teach well in a new medium. We hope that administrators as well as hands-on practitioners of online pedagogy will benefit from the experiences narrated in this book.

REFERENCES

Kim, K. -J., & Bonk, C. J. (2006). Online teaching and learning in higher education: The survey says... *Educause Quarterly* (4), 22–30.

Nassch, B. (1997). A brief history of distance education. Retrieved October 23, 2010 from http://www.scniornct.org/cdu/art/history.html

SECTION I

HUMANITIES

CHAPTER 2

TRANSFORMING A MEDIA STUDIES COURSE

Application of Asynchronous and Textual Technologies

Ian Reyes

This chapter details and evaluates the design and implementation of an online course in introductory media studies. Exploring the limits and potentials of asynchronous and textual course design for a small class, two key considerations for online teachers are discussed: timing and class size. In addition to technical matters, these two factors are found to be central to the design and implementation of an online course.

INTRODUCTION

Prior to my first experience teaching an online course, I worked for several semesters to incorporate online teaching elements into traditional, face-to-face teaching. The incremental approach to online teaching, transitioning one tool at a time until I was reasonably confident that I could run a course entirely online, made me more confident and competent than I would have been had I undertaken the project in one fell swoop. The Online Teaching Fellows program provided me with the additional knowledge and training

Taking Your Course Online: An Interdisciplinary Journey, pages 7–18
Copyright © 2012 by Information Age Publishing
All rights of reproduction in any form reserved.

to assure that my translated course met the standards of best practices for online teaching.

Nonetheless, acknowledging tacitly that online teaching differs from traditional teaching is quite different from turning that acknowledgment into an effective online class. In this chapter, I describe how a Media Studies course was converted for online teaching and how the implementation of that online curriculum played out during a ten-week summer course. First, I explain the rationale behind the (re)design of this course for an online course management system. Then, I explain and evaluate the implementation of that design. The sum of my experience is that online teaching has the potential to benefit instructors and students who are capable and willing to participate in a learning environment far more textual and asynchronous than more traditional settings.

ASYNCHRONOUS AND (HYPER)TEXTUAL

The course transformed was *Introduction to Broadcasting and Electronic Media*, a Freshman/Sophomore course for Communication Studies majors. The course was structured around Stanley J. Baran's (2008) *Introduction to Mass Communication: Media Literacy and Culture*. This was a natural choice because the original, face-to-face course already used the university's online course management system, WebCT, to host the syllabus, schedule, grade book, lecture slides, and an online discussion forum. The Baran text was also available as an e-book (offered through CourseSmart[1]) and was supplemented by an Online Learning Center (hosted by the original publisher, McGraw-Hill), offering study aids including glossaries and quizzes. This is to say that the tools for online teaching were pre-developed and tested, to an extent, in a regular, face-to-face context before going entirely online. Because the original course was a hybrid, by the time I took it online, there were few technical hurdles. In my situation, the main challenge was to figure out how best to use these proven tools to teach a course without face-to-face interaction. The most immediate concern on that front was planning for a situation that would be asynchronous and textual.

There is no technical reason this online course had to be either asynchronous or textual. The version of WebCT I was using supported real-time chat and upload/download of images and recorded audio/video files, but not live video or podcasting. Thus, asynchronicity and textuality were limits derived more from pedagogical than technological considerations.

Like many who have never taught online, I was most concerned about how to replace live lecture and discussion. Because the WebCT platform did not offer live audio/video streams, I considered finding a third-party solution that might allow an online class to meet in a virtual, multimedia classroom. But using real-time tools for an online course makes little sense, if you consider that one of the benefits sought by online students is flexible scheduling. Hosting synchronous group discussions or scheduling virtual office hours in a chat room imposes temporal demands that do not square with the scheduling needs online courses should be designed to satisfy. So, I came to focus on how best to conduct the course asynchronously.

Though WebCT did not have a podcast tool, I knew it was possible to upload and download recorded audio/video files to and from the WebCT page (which amounts to something like a podcast). This seemed like a reasonable alternative to lecturing, but the real issue was content. One idea was simply to record my face-to-face class, but my in-class lectures are more like discussions—contributions from students affect what and how I present course content—and there's no reason to believe listening-in on a face-to-face class will address the concerns and interests of another, online class. The other idea was to record MP3s of my own summaries and musings for each unit of the course, then post the files for students to download. Yet my concern was that this unidirectional model would be unlike talking directly with students in that it would encourage students to echo in their assignments whatever I said on the recording, rather than to think of their own responses to the course material.

So, considering that each unit of the course was well summarized by the textbook, the original slides from my face-to-face course, and the publisher's online supplements, the primary design problem for this course was how to solicit and organize student interaction in a primarily textual and asynchronous environment. With these considerations, the best tool and tactic for more student-centered online teaching turned out to be the discussion forum—basically a message board where students can post text and comment on others' posts. Nevertheless, to say that the course's environment was textual is not to say that the course content itself was limited to text, only that the primary delivery mechanism, or the central interface of the course management system, was limited to text. Because of the nature of course content concerning mass media, it was essential to integrate multimedia content somehow. For this, hypertext links to universal resource locators (URLs) were key. Using URLs was the easiest way to employ text within the core WebCT environment to link to multimedia from third-party sites.

Moreover, although the course was designed to be asynchronous, there were, nonetheless, scheduled due dates, although nothing required students and instructor to interact directly at a predetermined time. Carefully constructing a schedule is crucial for an online course. Consider that the weekly meetings of a face-to-face class set the pace and rhythm of the learning experience. While a degree of flexibility is, again, important for online students, it would be difficult to achieve asynchronous interaction of quality without certain deadlines defining each unit of the course.

SYLLABUS CHUNKING AND INTERFACE DESIGN

One of the most valuable concepts to come from the Online Teaching Fellows program, for me, was "chunking" a syllabus, or dividing it into units of ideas and activities. For adapting *Introduction to Broadcasting and Electronic Media*, I chunked the original syllabus into units consisting of one to two chapters from the textbook, a quiz, and a student contribution to the discussion forum. These were treated as sub-units leading to the final project: an individual research paper. First, I describe how each of these components were conceived. In the subsequent section, I describe how they functioned in practice.

Obviously, all courses consist of chunks; they're defined by a normal syllabus. There are readings to be done, for example, then quizzes about those readings, assignments applying the concepts from those readings, and so on. Then, the process repeats with the next unit. To take a course online, these activities, structured by the design of the syllabus, should become the guiding principle behind the design of the online course's interface.

The interface for my course site was as simple as possible: a main window where content appeared and, to the left of that window, a narrower navigation menu consisting of text links for each week/unit of the course, as well as links to other tools, like the syllabus and grade book. A click on "Unit 1," or any unit in the menu, revealed a submenu with each element to be completed that week: reading guide, glossary, quiz, and discussion forum. Each of these links activated the requisite tool in the main window or, for third-party tools, a pop-up window.

For each unit, I wrote a reading guide to the relevant sections of the textbook. Based on my lecture slides for the face-to-face course, the reading guides summarized key points and highlighted, in bulleted lists, central terms, ideas, and problems. These summaries were posted as .pdf files, which could be viewed online and/or downloaded, and each was linked to the "Reading Guide" in the unit submenu.[2] So, each week, the workflow for a student would begin with the reading guide, then proceed to the textbook readings for that unit, then reinforce that reading by reviewing the glossary, then go on to take the quiz and, finally, write in the discussion forum. Each unit sequence had to be completed during a one-week span running Monday through Sunday.

From the publisher's Online Learning Center, I used the glossary and quizzes. The glossary merely reflected the terms highlighted and defined in the textbook's glossary, so it was a redundant resource, included only to emphasize that I wanted students to be learning these terms and using them in the forum. The publisher's quiz tool, however, was a more valuable supplement.

Prior to the Fellows program, I did not think well of using quizzes for an online class. The usual face-to-face logic of a quiz—to spot-check students' understanding without the aid of references—just doesn't work for an online class. But, through the program, I realized that there is a place for quizzes in an online course, only their function is somewhat different from a traditional class. Quizzing may not be a good evaluative method for online teaching, but that does not mean it isn't a decent model for an interactive participation tool.

The multiple-choice quiz tool offered by the publisher automatically graded the work, provided feedback explaining why wrong answers were wrong, and allowed students to retake each quiz until they got everything correct. Even such a minimally interactive activity is, for online teaching, interaction of some value—if not as an evaluative tool, then as an automated substitute for face-to-face dialog aimed to reinforce retention of core vocabulary and concepts. In more quantitative terms, these quizzes, which, in principle, everyone should complete perfectly, were weighted only lightly, the same as in-class participation was in the face-to-face course. And the role of quizzes in the face-to-face grade distribution was replaced by short, weekly writing assignments for the online course.

In the face-to-face course, the online discussion forum was used to organize group projects. There, research groups worked out early drafts of their final presentation. For the online course, where a group presentation to the class would be impractical, I reconceived the discussion tool as a means for submitting writing assignments as well as engaging in asynchronous discussions.

Each discussion took place over two weeks and required a minimum of three contributions from each student. On Monday of the first week of a discussion, I created a new thread in the forum and gave the students a prompt. So, for instance, at the start of our two weeks on newspapers and magazines, the discussion prompt was: "How do you get your news? How do you think your experience of the news differs from that of people in past? What are some of the ways you see advertising and new media technologies affecting the form and content of the news you get?" In the first week of discussion, students posted their response to the prompts. In the second week of discussion, students wrote a minimum of two responses to the posts of their classmates. These discussions were evaluated based on a student's ability to apply key terms and concepts, to identify and explain relevant examples (which were usually illustrated by supplying a URL linked to an off-site media "text" of some sort, such as newspaper articles or YouTube videos) and to advance the discussion by introducing new ideas and examples (rather than repeating other people's contributions or merely stating agreement/disagreement).

In addition to the brief writing done for the discussion forum, students were also required to work on a research paper over the course of the semester. This type of assignment required no significant adaptation for the online course: students simply emailed their proposals, drafts, and final essays rather than submitting paper. Because I knew from requiring students to submit work via email in the past that different file formats could be a problem, I was sure to require all work be submitted as a .doc or .docx file. This was partly to make sure that I could decode their files, and partly because Microsoft Word's "Insert Comment" tool is, in my opinion, a great way to mark-up essays electronically.

Aside from these matters, there's a final meta-issue to consider: how to deploy each of these units with regard to the course schedule. Since I was anticipating my first try at online teaching to be labor intensive, I completed all of the design for the course site, covering all ten weeks, before the summer session started. Yet from more experienced online teachers, I found that this could backfire if I were to publish all ten weekly units on the first day of the class. That is, setting due dates to discourage procrastination is only one half of the scheduling issue; the other is pacing the release of content so that students can't rush to complete the requirements for the entire semester in the first week, which is probably not best for the learner, and is certainly a detriment to any effort to coordinate interaction between students throughout the course (as with the discussion forum I intended to use). With this in mind, though the units were entirely assembled before the first day of class, I published each to the course web site only one week ahead of schedule. So, though the syllabus spelled out what was to be covered and when, students could not submit work more than one week ahead due to the regulated release of each chunk of the course.

IMPLEMENTATION

One week prior to the start of the semester, I sent an email to all enrolled students introducing myself and the course. Since this online class was scheduled for a somewhat accelerated ten-week summer session, it was important to start immediately. Likewise, it was also reasonable to believe that some of the students would be new to online courses. With that in mind, the first email contact included the syllabus as well as a statement regarding the technological requirements and responsibilities for online students. The statement read:

> Because this is an online course, you are expected to own and maintain a working computer, email account, and internet connection. Further, you are expected to know how to use these technologies. The instructor's role is not to

provide technical support. Technical problems will not be accepted as excuses for late/missing assignments. Therefore, it is also recommended that you have a backup plan in case you encounter technical issues during this course.

Aside from these basic access requirements, however, I did not assume students would be familiar with specific course management tools. While some tools, like the grade book and syllabus, were self-explanatory, others requiring interaction, like the quizzes and discussion forum, called for explanation.

Through a rubric on the course web site, quizzes were explained in terms of their role in each unit and their weight in the grade distribution. I was also sure to emphasize that, because the quizzes were hosted by a third-party, students would have to be sure to use the "Email Results" link at the end of each quiz, otherwise I would have no official record of the results. Additional technical instructions for using the quiz tool were offered through the publisher's Online Learning Center.

For introducing the discussion tool, the introductory email called for an (ungraded) assignment to introduce oneself to the class via discussion forum within the first week. This would help to see who was really "there" and to allow us to get a sense for one another's personalities and interests before the academic discussions began. It was also intended to ensure that students understood how to use the forum tool and how to work with the architecture of the thread/post/comment system. In a large class, an online discussion forum can become unwieldy if students don't submit their required assignments to the correct section of the forum. This I knew from using such forums in hybrid courses. As it turned out, however, managing a large online class was not a problem I would face.

The spring semester face-to-face course upon which the online summer class was based was fully enrolled, with thirty students. One week before the online course started, when I sent the introductory email, twelve people were enrolled. Only ten were still enrolled on day one of the summer session. Of those ten, eight did the introduction assignment through the discussion forum. Of the two who did not, one dropped soon after and the other remained on the roster for the semester but never logged on. A third student dropped by mid-semester (after she was caught plagiarizing), which left only seven active students by semester's end.

This means my assessment of the course design explained above is based on a very limited application. Clearly, my experience was defined by a small group of individuals. Nonetheless, there are two conclusions I feel comfortable drawing. First, the course design I've explained is not optimized for a small class: its model of "discussion" presumes a critical mass of participants. Without such mass, the next best thing, I found, is a few strong voices. Second, this model of online teaching overwhelmingly favors students who are highly literate and self-motivated; it may be that this model calls for a level of competency even higher than do most face-to-face courses. Yet none of this is to say that anything went drastically wrong. In fact, most aspects of the course worked perfectly. But there's some obvious room for improvement.

Of the things that went well, the syllabus, grade book, and grading rubrics were the best. There were surprisingly few questions about when things were due, what their grades were, or why their grades were so. Some students still missed deadlines for discussions and quizzes, which was expected. What I did not expect, however, was that some students would submit their quizzes on time but with incorrect answers. Though I had explained in the quiz rubric that quizzes count for credit and that there is no reason to get less than a perfect score (because it is "open book" and because the tool allows users to re-take the quizzes before submitting), some students nonetheless chose to submit less than perfect results (and receive less than perfect scores). The same was true for the discussions, where participation, in most cases, tended toward the absolute minimum.

As with most students for any course, students in this online class tended to submit their work at the last minute. Because I scheduled each unit for one week running from 12:01am Monday to Sunday at midnight, nearly everything everyone did for every unit was submitted between noon and midnight Sunday. Regardless, the timing was not a problem in terms of the quality of interaction (though it made for a lopsided working week on my end). What did become a problem for the students was the effect that minimal or missing contributions would have on the overall quality of the discussion forum as a learning experience.

No one posted more frequently to the discussion forum than was required; nearly half contributed less frequently than required. Moreover, as with the quizzes, although the criteria for full credit were spelled out in a rubric, some students chose to contribute less. With larger numbers, this trend, which I found also in my hybrid courses, is negligible. With a large enough group, this kind of assignment, even with uneven participation, still exposes students to a wide range of ideas and provides them with a good amount of peer feedback (not to mention the experience of being the one providing that feedback). It also gives me a good sense of how they understand the material. With less than ten students and less than total commitment to the course, however, this was not so. What I wound up with was, for lack of a better classification, some strong voices, a wallflower, and two chronically confused voices.

The strong voices included students with vested interests in a certain area of media studies (a web designer and an aspiring journalist) and some who just had axes to grind (a self-described cultural conservative and a student who related virtually everything to the war in Iraq). Without this cadre, the forum would have been a mere formality and not a discussion in any meaningful sense. There was just enough interest and diversity among these four, constituting the majority of the class, to carry something like a conversation throughout the semester, but it was obvious to me that there was not as much substance to the conversation as there could be.

If there were, for example, ten or fifteen strong voices in a group, there would be a good amount of thoughtful content generated over the course of a discussion. With the discussion requirements calling for one original post and two pieces of feedback from each student, lines of thinking can be significantly expanded and refined through dialectics spreading across dozens of contributions. With at most a dozen strong contributions over the course of two weeks, however, I found that the online class discussions weren't coming close to addressing the same amount of material the face-to-face course did, or a more populated online course would.

The wallflower contributed as if he had read through the rubrics and was determined to do only enough to assure a C, which, for all I know, is true and, honestly, fine by me, except that, again, in a small group, even a little non-participation has a big impact. More worrisome were the two students I can best describe politely as confused. Simply put, they seemed to be trying harder than the wallflower but were such terrible writers that their contributions were difficult, if not impossible, to understand. Further, their contributions made it clear that they were also having trouble reading; they were not applying basic terms and concepts correctly and could not supply coherent feedback to their classmates' posts. By midterm, it was plain to see that these two were floundering and that they were being ignored by the strong voices.

So, in this situation, I was confronted with two problems. One was that the majority of students, who were putting in a solid effort and getting decent results, were still not getting the breadth and depth of experience for which I was aiming. The other problem was the schism resulting from these students ostracizing those who were openly struggling. Neither problem was easy to solve, and I can't say I completely fixed either of them. For both, the central question was when and how often to intervene in the forum myself.

In an ideal situation, writing in a discussion forum should elevate the overall quality of student work and, among the strong voices, I definitely noticed a general improvement in the writing and critical thinking skills demonstrated in the forum over the course of the semester. The trouble, to my mind, was that they simply couldn't generate enough content among themselves to think critically about. Knowing from the face-to-face course the potential range of discussion on these topics, there were some examples, arguments, and issues that I noticed going unmentioned in the limited discussions within this small group. For example, considering that this is supposed to be an introduction to media studies, how long should I let a discussion about the internet continue without a mention of the "digital divide"? Though it's mentioned in the textbook, is that enough? If the students don't take interest in it, should I take it upon myself to inject it into their forum? If I do decide to introduce the issue myself, when do I do it?

Consider also that, with the trend toward submitting work at the last minute, there weren't many natural points to intervene. With students almost universally posting their feedback to one another within the last hours before the due date, there wasn't really a stream of conversation I could slip into. Instead, it was more like two blasts: one, an opening salvo of initial replies to a discussion topic and, two, the last-minute volley of peer feedback. With this, my options were to interject after the first blast, saying my piece about how I'd like the rest of the conversation to go, or to comment after the second blast about the important things I felt were missing from the thread.

I attempted both strategies and wasn't totally satisfied with the results of either. Intervening before students wrote their feedback resulted in nearly all of them addressing exactly and only what I mentioned in my comments. But when commenting after the fact, I honestly didn't know if any of them read what I wrote. The closest to a solution I found was to respond to each original post with a series of questions that could help expand upon the students' initial ideas. Being conscientious about representing what I considered to be a good range of content through my feedback, and knowing that most of the students' feedback would faithfully address whatever I suggested, meant that I could, essentially, force the discussion to go where I thought it should. Still, this was an awkward and artificial means of achieving what, in another situation with a larger class, should have happened organically.

The other problem of students having trouble reading and writing was more intractable. The obvious Catch-22 was in helping someone who is having trouble reading one thing (the text) by giving them something else to read (my feedback). Worse was how to tell if their understanding improves when the only way to convey understanding is through writing, which they're also struggling with. I tried to reply to their forum posts with shorter, simpler, and more direct feedback than the others, but the quality of their contributions remained the same. I also replied, privately, with recommendations to seek help from the University's Academic Enhancement Center before attempting to do their final research papers for the course. I have no idea whether they sought help, but I ultimately saw the same poor work in their final papers despite doing what I could to help them through the proposal and draft phases of the project. As for the strong voices in the class, their final projects were quite good. In fact, I'd say that they were better than what I usually get from face-to-face classes, and one paper in particular was among the best I've ever seen from a Freshman/Sophomore level student. So, in the end, the textual and asynchronous design of this online course appeared to be a considerable challenge to some students but a major benefit to others.

REFLECTIONS

From a technical standpoint, an online course like this—asynchronous, heavily textual, and supplemented by third-party content—could be well run using virtually any online course management system or even a regular blogging application. While it would be nice if students could contribute something other than text, doing so would require the right tools, knowledge, and resources—technical requirements that must either be taught within the online course or spelled-out as prerequisite skills and materials. Barring that, one is left with the limitations of text-based, asynchronous online discussions progressing slowly and, though capable of fostering more refined thinking, addressing only a limited amount of course material (especially with an unusually small class). Still, the students adapted to the technical limitations of the discussion board by consistently supplying URLs to ready-made multimedia content. Including URLs within the online discussion forum was not a required part of class participation, but it became the norm. I saw this emergent standard in both the spring semester hybrid and summer online courses. The practice mirrors plainly the kind of link sharing and commenting found in social media like Facebook and Twitter. It turned out to be such an effective way of maximizing on the limitations of the course management software and of extending the virtual classroom that, now, I require it in the online writing assignments for my face-to-face courses.

From a pedagogical standpoint, online teaching, as I implemented it, involves an unusual amount of writing for both the instructor and the students, an amount far exceeding that required for face-to-face classes. Between email correspondence, assignments, discussions, rubrics, and directions for each component of the course, the bulk of my labor was writing. Of course, for students, this also meant careful reading and writing were essential for the successful completion of this course. Those entering with strong literacy skills were at a clear advantage and, in my estimation, may have learned more from this online course than they would have from the less textual, face-to-face class. Those with weak literacy were at a disadvantage and probably would have fared better in a more traditional, oral, face-to-face setting.

On the whole, I don't believe this would have gone as smoothly if I had not already taught this course as a hybrid. I highly recommend that anyone interested in online teaching approach the project incrementally by first adding online components to a face-to-face course. In my experience, being well versed in online teaching technologies allowed me to focus more on pedagogical matters, which, in sum, are found where diverse learning styles meet technological limits.

Above and beyond tools and content, timing should be considered a major factor in online course design. Along with pacing the release of syllabus chunks, managing due dates is important to creating and sustaining quality interaction through tools like discussion forums. I believe that I would have had different results had I released all content at once, at the beginning of the course, or released it more slowly during the semester. Further, I'm confident that the problem of last-minute submissions negatively affecting student interaction in the discussion forum could be solved by dividing the course into different sections with different, staggered due dates so that, even if everyone contributes only at the last minute, they will do so at different times, permitting the discussion to evolve more slowly and allowing more natural points for instructors to intervene. These are just a few, basic strategies concerned with pacing. To be sure, there's room for considerable micromanagement on this front.

The other, far less controllable, factor is class size. Particularly when a course is designed to solicit interaction, the number of students one has to engage impacts the efficacy of interactive design strategies. Faced with low enrollment, my application of the discussion tool, which worked well in larger hybrid courses, did not work as well with a much smaller group. Unable to rely on these discussions to cover content in a more organic, self-directed manner, I had to take a more authoritarian and one-on-one approach to online class discussion. So, I found, when designing an online course, that class size should be anticipated as a major factor affecting the efficacy of certain pedagogical strategies. To the extent that enrollment is predictable, instructors should plan accordingly and, considering the extent to which it is unpredictable, planning accordingly means leaving room to reconsider the course's design during its implementation.

NOTES

1. CourseSmart is a service managing online distribution of e-book permissions for academic publishers (available at http://www.coursesmart.com/).
2. The benefit of .pdf format is that, unlike .doc files, for example, a .pdf is more like a picture of a text than an actual text file and, therefore, is a more reliable way to ensure a document will correctly display the intended formatting when students view it. Further, unlike .html format, which can equally control for how a file is displayed, .pdf files are more easily downloaded for offline viewing.

REFERENCES

Baran, S. J. (2008). *Introduction to mass communication: Media literacy and culture* (5th ed.). New York: McGraw-Hill.

CHAPTER 3

TOWARD UNIVERSAL DESIGN IN LEARNING

Converting a Writing/Disability Studies Course From Physical to Virtual Space

Celest Martin

This chapter narrates the transformation of a Writing course in Disability Studies from its first offering as a face-to-face course to a summer online offering. I detail the advantages and disadvantages of both formats as I experienced them, and provide recommendations for those wishing to perform a similar conversion. In addition, I offer suggestions specific to writing teachers, while embracing the universal access enabled by the online environment.

"I've been wanting to take that course, but it's always scheduled when I have to work."

"I'm trying to take all my classes at our city campus this semester. I don't want to drive down to the main campus 45 minutes each way just for one class, but it's a requirement."

"The winters are harsh where I live. Getting around a hilly campus in a motorized chair when it's icy and snowy isn't something I choose to do. So I take all my courses in the summer and fall. There's a few courses I'd like to take,

Taking Your Course Online: An Interdisciplinary Journey, pages 19–34
Copyright © 2012 by Information Age Publishing
All rights of reproduction in any form reserved.

though, that are offered only during the winter semester. And I'd finish my degree faster if I could take them then."

"I'd like to teach a summer course, but I can't physically be on-campus because of my research. I'm spending much of the summer visiting archives."

Well folks, welcome to the online classroom! Now we can offer students courses in the comfort of their homes, dorm rooms, apartments, or favorite WiFi cafés. And we can teach them from our preferred spaces. But are the experiences comparable? Is teaching a class conventionally—in physical space—and teaching it virtually—wherever one wishes —the same? Is one better than the other? Let's just say they're different, each with their own advantages. Below is the story of one course, taught both ways. It is a writing course, within a writing major, specifically WRT 306: *Writing Health and Disability*.

WRT 306: ITS PLACE IN OUR CURRICULUM

For the general student population, *Writing Health and Disability* is an elective for anyone who wishes to take it. For Writing majors, it is one of five courses in our "300" series. Students must choose at least four of these courses to fulfill the requirements for the Writing major. The courses in this series all fulfill general education requirements, and are configured to emphasize social ends to writing. The other courses are:

- WRT 302: *Writing Culture*
- WRT 303: *Writing for Community Service*
- WRT 304: *Public Writing*
- WRT 305: *Travel Writing*

Prior to the WRT 306 online offering, both WRT 302 and WRT 305 had been offered regularly online. At the time of the transformation of WRT 306 to an online offering, both the University of Rhode Island and the Writing and Rhetoric Program wanted to expand their online offerings, hoping to attract new students, and to enhance accessibility for the students we already had. As the designer of this course, I felt particularly strongly about offering *Writing Health and Disability* in both formats: a course about disability should certainly be accessible to all.

TEACHING WRT 306 FACE-TO-FACE

For the students present on that clear, blue sky September day in the fall of 2008, WRT 306 was the first class they had ever taken related to disability. Some lived with their own disabilities, or with those of friends or family members. These students had an easier time with the first assignment, the personal narrative experience with disability. However, when it came to treating disability as an academic subject, acknowledging *Disability Studies* as a field with strong theoretical underpinnings, and placing their new knowledge within a rhetorical framework, no student had an advantage over the other. This was a new experience for all. As such, it was a heavy reading, discussion-intensive class. In fact, because the students were absorbing content so new to them, and in some cases theoretically dense, it was a challenge to keep the course placed firmly within the major, by additionally focusing on rhetorical frameworks and writing skills.

So how did I teach it?

The course included two theoretical texts:

- *Embodied Rhetorics: Disability in Language and Culture* (Wilson & Lewiecki-Wilson, 2001)
- *Disability Discourse: Disability, Human Rights, and Society* (Corker & French, 1999)

Two first person narratives:

- *Homebound: Growing Up with a Disability in America* (Irvin, 2004)
- *Being with Rachel* (Brennan, 2002)

Two policy texts:

- *Disabling Interpretations: The Americans with Disabilities Act in Federal Court* (Mezey, 2005)
- *Writing Public Policy* (Smith, 2005) (skills text)

In addition to reading the texts, the course required a considerable investment of time from the students in the following areas: researching the discursive practices surrounding disability in our culture (examining song lyrics, poetry, films, TV programs, etc.), finding venues for possible publication of the two cultural critiques required, and collaborating on the public policy assignment.

The course was ambitious to teach, and arduous to take because of the wide variety of writing styles expected from the students, in addition to exposure to content not covered in other writing classes. Understanding this content required mastering new terminology and unpacking the theoretical readings, both on my own part, and on the part of the students. In this regard, the two narratives assigned were helpful, because they provided the students lived accounts of disability in narrative form, thus offering them models for their own narratives, and serving as *praxis* with which to connect the theory.

Because of the unique demands of the course, and the fact that I had hoped to show at least one full-length film, some film clips, as well as clips from *YouTube,* I had requested a once-a-week, three-hour format. Unfortunately, the class was scheduled in a three times a week in a 50-minute time frame. The scheduling made it difficult, on occasion, to accomplish all that we needed to. The class nearly always ran over, and students felt frustrated. Towards the end of the course, students told me they were circulating a petition to the Director of Writing and Rhetoric to offer the class in the seminar format next time around. I mention this because time frame was an important consideration when converting the course to an online offering.

Course goals included the following:

- To articulate some of the ways in which disability is represented in our culture, both positively, and negatively
- To define "disability discourse" and "disability culture"
- To write about disability in a way that is personally meaningful, and publicly informative; in other words, to construct a disability narrative that takes readers to a place they have not yet explored
- To understand disability policies as they exist in our culture, and as they *should* exist in our culture.
- To craft disability policy

WHAT WE DID IN CLASS

In class, as in every writing class, we had peer review sessions for the written work. Depending on the assignment, students worked in pairs or in groups to critique each others' work. The criteria for evaluation of the work changed with each piece, depending on purpose and audience for the writing, and was presented to the class on handouts. There were five writing assignments: two cultural critiques (essentially persuasive), one narrative, one collaborative public policy assignment, and one eight to ten page piece in a genre of the student's choice. This last piece was not due in final form until the day of the final exam, when writing portfolios are traditionally collected, in accordance with department programmatic guidelines. In addition to peer-reviewing each individual assignment, students also spent a class period working one-on-one to review one another's portfolios. (The final portfolio consists of three of the four shorter assignments, chosen by the student and revised in accordance with feedback, their long piece, and a reflective cover letter.)

On days when students were not working on writing assignments, we had guided discussion of the readings. There was usually no difficulty in motivating students to discuss their readings, as the content and ideas of disability rights and disability activism, while new to them, were comparable to issues of civil rights they discussed in sociology, history, or even psychology classes. I was fortunate to have a very cohesive class of 20, one of those groups of students with a gift-like intensity of purpose. I remember I always left that class smiling.

Because of this tight-knit cohesion, students had little difficulty with the final, collaborative project, resulting in a public policy document. Those who do collaborative work in their classrooms know that it can be fraught with perils and contention. This time, it wasn't. The assignment required students to seek out issues of accessibility on campus, and to work in groups to propose a solution for the problem to the appropriate campus body. "The Elevator Coalition," "The Committee for Accessible Dormitories," and the "Campus Transportation Committee" are examples of the way students grouped themselves. These students worked longer and harder to produce a product than had ever been my experience in 30 years of teaching. They were permitted to choose the best format for their product from their *Writing Public Policy* (Smith, 2005) book. Some chose petitions; others, the "Recommendations for Policy Changes" format; and others wrote new policy. They made multiple copies of their work for the various vice-presidents of the university under whose aegis their plan fell, and for the head of Disability Services. It was one of those assignments that worked so well that the students' dedication brought tears to my eyes. As such, when I converted to an online course, I brainstormed ways to replicate this assignment.

FINAL EXAM

The students' take-home final examination consisted of their reflective cover-letter for their portfolios. In this cover letter, they were asked to do the following:

- Introduce each piece (citing, for example, what compelled them to write the piece)
- Reflect upon what revisions they made and why
- Examine shifts in their attitudes toward disability over the course of the semester
- Reflect upon their growth as writers, peer-reviewers, observers of culture, and as knowledgeable and purposeful rhetoricians

ddition to this take-home final examination, the actual time period final (three hours) was allotted for groups to present their accessibility study and resulting policies. Since we had an 8:00 AM final, I supplied coffee, juice, muffins and bagels, and we had a productive and interesting discussion of the many shortcomings of the campus in meeting Americans with Disabilities Act (ADA) requirements. Students were quite knowledgeable about the ADA at this point, because we had a guest speaker from the Governor's Commission on Disability who discussed the ADA in full during our unit on accessibility.

THE TRANSFORMATION: WHAT CHANGES DID I MAKE?

When our Provost's office offered stipends for those who had no experience with online teaching, but were willing to engage in a semester-long workshop to learn how to do so, and commit to offering an online course in the summer following the workshop, I was thrilled with the opportunity. Although several people in my program had offered online courses, I had been unsuccessful in gaining access to their expertise. *Writing Health and Disability* was the course I chose because I believed passionately that it should be accessible to all who wanted to take it. The workshop leaders were extraordinary in their ability to help us imagine what areas of our courses would need special attention in the conversion process. One of the things they stressed was an initial caveat to students about online courses, reminding them that they were "real" courses. My caveat to students looked like this:

About Taking an Online-Course: You can take an-online course in your pajamas, but you can't sleep through it! Keeping up with an online course requires self-discipline. Here are some things to keep in mind:

- *You need to check the course web site Sundays through Thursdays.* (EVERY Sunday through Thursday). I may have added new information about an assignment, or discovered something I want to link you to (a newspaper or magazine article; a documentary or news piece on television).
- *I will not be checking course web site on Fridays or Saturdays,* so don't expect replies to posts or e-mails then. If there is a special assignment coming up that I think is particularly difficult, you can ask me if I am available on Saturday to help. Otherwise, I will begin checking responses again on Sunday evening.
- *You will be reading each other's work online.* You may find it helpful at times to *print out hard copies of your classmates' work,* and read them

closely and carefully so that you can provide the kind of constructive feedback that will be valuable to your classmates. You will receive more information on how to collaborate in an online group and how to provide feedback later.

- You will need to *keep up with the readings and post your responses to them on the dates listed* in order to receive credit for the posting. Written assignments will also be due on the dates listed. You need to remember that I cannot possibly read and evaluate all of your work during the last week of class. Due dates are firm so that I have the time to read your work and evaluate it in the ways that will be most helpful and meaningful to you.

- When you post responses to your readings, *I will also ask that you respond to others' posts about the readings.* It's a conversation, just as we would have if we were sitting in the classroom. Feel free to disagree with others and with me, but remember to follow the rules of web etiquette that you would on any listserv.

- You will be *evaluating your classmates' work online.* Generally, I will assign the writers to whom you should respond, so that I can make sure everyone gets a response. You will need to check for your assigned groups or partners, (depending on the assignment) online.

- There is a *collaborative assignment* in this class. Although you will be doing field research for this assignment independently, you will pool your results online to make collaborative recommendations. This is your policy assignment, and you will receive more information about this later.

- *Communication* with me is important. If you are having difficulty with an assignment, whether it is writing an essay or grasping the readings, you will have to let me know. You can certainly send me a private detailed e-mail and I will help.

- *Keep up!* It is easy to get the illusion that this is not a "real" class, and to forget after a long day at work, or an afternoon on the beach, that you need to come home and check your online course to be sure you are up-to-date and have completed all required assignments by the specified date.

In addition, I supplied a rubric for evaluating online posts (Table 3.1). I had never supplied a "discussion rubric," for a face-to-face class, rather only a paragraph on the syllabus detailing all that was required in "class participation." Such a detailed rubric for discussion was new to me.

TABLE 3.1 Rubric for Evaluating Posts in the Online Version of WRT 306—*Writing Health and Disability*

Grade	Evidence of close reading of assigned texts	Criteria		
		Demonstrates how reading reinforces or refutes own experience with disability	Provides evidence of original insight gained from the mix of readings with own experience	Engages with other student in class
A	Refers to text and evaluates statements by bringing in outside material	Integrates own experience with disability thoughtfully with the readings	Provides explanation of how she arrived at original insight ("ah-ha" moment)	Engages with at least two other posts for every reading; demonstrates back and forth flow of conversation
B	Refers to text and evaluates statements	Connects reading and experiences less directly	Discusses readings, but does not provide any fresh insights	Responds to others, but does not engage classmates in conversational flow
C	Writes generally about the reading but does not refer to the text at all	Goes off on tangent of own experience, disconnected from the text	Provides original insight, but is not clear how he arrived at this insight	Fails to respond to the posts of other students.

THE ONLINE EXPERIENCE

Did everything go as smoothly as I'd hoped for my online version? Of course not. Despite the fact that the books and an extended course description had been posted nearly a month in advance, students did not all begin the course with the books. Since the books were not available at a University bookstore, students had to order them from the vendor of their choice. I did not have the right to insist that they pay the extra shipping costs associated with express delivery; the best I could do was recommend that if they could afford it, they use this option. As for the films, I left it up to the students whether to rent or buy them. None complained of any difficulty.

I began the course with 12 students, a nice number for a summer course. When the first posts were due, only eight responded, despite the fact that I made sure to ask questions that didn't yet require any reading, to allow for the late acquisition of books. I sent a reminder to the late posters immediately; both thanked me. One posted immediately; the other delayed. I felt frustrated that I couldn't "speak" to this student, and let him know that he was not off to a good start. I had to take a deep breath, remind myself I had done all I could do, and that, as in any other class, the rest was up to him. I received an e-mail from one of the students who dropped, explaining "there was too much reading and writing" for a summer course, and it would interfere with his job. OK, his choice. I reminded myself that students dropped all the time in face-to-face courses, and the drop rate was usually higher in the summer.

By the second week, students had introduced themselves, and some give-and-take began to occur on the discussion forum. What was interesting was that it was just as easy to spot my "best" student online as it was in a face-to-face class. His prose was engaging and enthusiastic, and I could feel an immediate connection. Unlike some of the others, whose introductions were stilted, his was conversational, and other-directed.

Because the class was so small, I abandoned the idea of having them work in groups for peer review, as is usual in writing classes, and everyone posted their papers for all to see and critique. I posted the same guidelines for writing and critiquing each assignment as I had used in my classroom course.

It turned out that the second week of class contained the most popular of the online assignments. This assignment required the students to post links to song lyrics containing references to mental illness. The links flew back and forth, with students commenting in lively fashion on songs they hadn't realized were about depression, for example. One of these was Sarah Maclachlan's "In the Arms of an Angel," one of my contributions. So exciting was this conversation that I stayed up till 1:00 AM one morning, involved in this intense discussion. I found out (as I should have known, having raised two teen-agers) that the kids really came alive late at night. Unfortunately, at 58,

I no longer do. Consequently, I was unable to engage in most of these late-night "conversations," though I managed it one or two other times.

HOW I TAUGHT

Every week, I posted discussion questions related to the readings. Only a few students answered these in the depth I would like to have seen and engaged with other posts. Engaging with the posts of others when it came to the readings seemed to be one of the most difficult requirements for the students. Some, week-after week, dutifully answered the questions but didn't bother to respond to their classmates' posts. The "Tracking" tool allowed me to see that one or two students were logging on to the site far more times than they were posting to it, and this puzzled me. I couldn't understand why they would bother to log on, but ignore my repeated references to the rubric and reminders that they needed to engage in conversation with others. Once again, inability to speak directly with the students frustrated me.

One popular feature I used in the online course was a weekly bonus question. Each question was worth one point, and students who answered all ten would have ten points added to their participation (posting) grade. While only one student succeeded in garnering all 10 points, the "bonus question" appeared to generate some competition, and some additional posts. To answer the question, students generally need only to search a term, or a reference. The questions related to the week's discussion topics, and perhaps the most popular bonus questions occurred during film weeks. The films themselves generated more posts than did discussion questions based on the readings. (Should we be surprised at that? I think not!)

Because some of the readings were dense and somewhat theoretical, I found that I had to supply a great deal of background information in the form of "content modules." These modules contained information that I would have presented orally in the face-to-face class. This piece of the course—gauging how much "extra" information the students needed to process the readings—was difficult. In part, this difficulty occurred because the students did not ask questions of me about the readings as they did in the classroom (although I encouraged them to do so). I had to guess about what might be brand new information for them, and about their ability to process the material.

THE COLLABORATIVE POLICY PIECE: NOT

I gave up on doing the policy piece collaboratively. While my original plan had been that students would gather information either around their college campus or in their community concerning accessibility issues, and then come together in small groups to pool their information and write one policy piece, in the end it just didn't seem feasible. I had one student at the URI campus, a young man in Chicago, a young lady in New York, and students at various points in between. Their interests in accessibility varied widely, and for some reason, they never got around to ordering the little *Writing Public Policy* book. In addition, I was unable to provide them with the guest speaker who had been so helpful in our face-to-face class. (Not that doing so would have been an impossibility in virtual space; I simply didn't plan far enough ahead.) In the end, I settled for their each writing a paper discussing some aspect of accessibility. After the tremendous success of the collaborative project on the accessibility issue project in the face-to-face class, I was disappointed with myself for not being able to make it work in cyberspace.

OPPORTUNITIES AND LIMITATIONS IN TEACHING *WRITING HEALTH AND DISABILITY* ONLINE

The greatest opportunities offered by conversion to an online course were these:

- My students and I would no longer be bound by what could happen in 50 minutes, 75 minutes, or even 3 hours.
- Discussion could continue unfettered by clocks.
- We could watch as many *YouTube* clips as we wanted, when we wanted. Students could take more time with peer-review.
- I could organize my time so that working through every summer weekend would not be a necessity, but rather an option when I thought students needed extra help.
- My "posting rubric" would make plain their obligations to students and I wouldn't have to repeat myself *ad infinitum* as in the classroom, because everything was in writing in one place. My assumption was that students wouldn't lose handouts and syllabi as they tended to do in face-to-face classes not accompanied by a companion website. Students could refer to announcements, modules, rubrics, and due dates whenever they wished.

Of all of these issues, I would say that peer reviewing was perhaps the greatest beneficiary of cyberspace. Students seemed less concerned with hurting classmates' feelings than in a face-to-face class, and more invested in getting their fellow writers to express themselves clearly, providing missing information and sensory detail. This was a great boon. Students hearing directly from other students in writing about the strengths and weaknesses of their work contributed to more substantive revisions.

In addition, students seemed to enjoy the challenge of posting links to film reviews, song lyrics, poems, and *YouTube* clips concerned with disability. They engaged in this activity over the whole course, rather than doing it for only one class as they had when we met in the classroom. Consequently, all of us were exposed to a greater variety of media relevant to the subject matter than we otherwise would have been.

MYTHS, REALITIES, AND LIMITATIONS

Several elements made my first online offering less than ideal. For one thing, it was a summer offering. Rightly or wrongly, students have come to expect that summer school is a little bit easier. My course is a tough one, a course for those truly committed to writing, Disability Studies, or both. Out of my 12 initial students, only one fit the profile of the "truly committed." In the end, only seven students actually completed the course satisfactorily. Despite my repeated reminders concerning the number of posts for which they were responsible (reminders I assumed I wouldn't have to issue, given the very clear rubric), some students simply ignored me, and one tried to make up all his posts in the last week, despite my caveat in my initial message to the students, "About Taking An Online Course." Another student e-mailed and apologized, claiming that he thought the course was for only five weeks (the usual term of a summer course) and that he had an internship in New York City for the second five weeks, and simply couldn't keep up. He did, however, remain in the course, and made a valiant effort.

So, logistics. Before actually examining those elements of the course affected by cyberspace, I'd like to comment on the two constraints imposed on it simply as a result of timing. First, the course was offered in summer session, which by its very nature holds different expectations for both students and faculty. Secondly, while our face-to-face summer courses are offered in an intensive five-week slot, our online courses bridge both summer sessions, for a total of ten weeks. What I and several of my colleagues found, however, was that ten weeks was too long in the summer. Not only was it difficult to sustain the momentum of the course (posts grew more and more infrequent toward the end), but other students, like mine, genuinely believed upon signing up that because the course began the day after Commencement, it would end in five weeks.

As far as limitations imposed by the online format, I would say they fell into the following categories:

- Discussion
- Collaborative Work
- Knowledge of appropriate interventions to take and when

Discussion revolving around the readings and back-and-forth communication was less than in my face-to-face class. Of course, as students dropped from 12 to eight, there were far fewer enrolled than would be in a course offered during the regular semester (usually 22). Two students were excellent respondents, representing 25% of the population, about the norm for any class of the truly outstanding. Still, I believe I could do a better job at this aspect of the course if I were to have the opportunity again. Nevertheless, the limitation imposed by not seeing faces in front of me will probably always be a factor for someone as people-oriented as I am.

As I mentioned earlier, my failure at the collaborative assignment rankled me. The limitation here was that students were not able to form groups who could assess accessibility in the same physical space *together*. I had originally planned to inquire whether any students lived in proximity to one another and see if I could organize the assignment that way. However, I was advised that this was not a hybrid course, and such a technique would not be appropriate. I suppose I could devise a different kind of collaborative policy piece, and in fact would do so if I were to offer the course online again. I would simply have to make the policy piece more theoretical; in other words, posing questions such as "What features should a Universally Designed dormitory have?" Students could research Universal Design and devise a policy collaboratively, rather than visiting physical spaces together.

Finally, perhaps the greatest limitation imposed by the online environment is the inability to see body language, to read those subtle signs that suggest whether students are "getting it" or struggling. My guess is that if one were teaching non-traditionally-aged students, they might be more forthcoming with questions when they are confused than the 18–22 year-old age group. But although I made a great effort to define terms I used in my posts and to suggest links leading to easy-to-understand information to supplement the readings, I concluded that most members of the online class did not make the same gains in understanding disability in all of its contexts as my face-to-face class, with, of course, the usual one or two exceptions. This element—lack of nonverbal feedback—remains a conundrum. In the classroom, I make sure the students understand I am a very accessible professor, that they may come to my office nearly any time for clarification. Most choose to e-mail with questions about the readings and about assignments, but several still take advantage of face-to-face contact. The problem I found with the online class is that they didn't even e-mail with questions. I'm not sure they knew what they didn't know! Engaging students more fully, and re-enacting the same kind of dialogue online as we

om remains a challenge I would face. Next time, perhaps
vantage of the "Chat" tool, holding online office hours to
night yield.

‹ WRITING TEACHERS: HOW I EVALUATED THE PAPERS

Just a quick note on the physicality of reading the students' papers and
providing them with feedback: I found it unpleasant to use the "Comment"
function of my word processing program on papers, as this required sitting
at the computer for hours and made me feel compelled me to revert to
correcting every single error—the old "shotgun approach"—something I
abandoned well over 30 years ago. Instead, I printed the papers out, making extensive notes to myself on the back of them. Each student then received a detailed page or two of comments, referring to particular lines
when necessary. They loved this form of feedback and, with one exception,
all provided revisions to their work in accordance with both their peers'
and my feedback. As noted earlier, revision tended to be more substantive
than in the face-to-face class, and this certainly was a boon.

RECOMMENDATIONS

- If you don't know how to do something on your course web site,
  speak up! Find out who else is using it, get together with them, and
  get help. Don't begin your course feeling anything less that 100% confident about handling whatever course shell your University is using.
- I do recommend rubrics for evaluation of posts, tests, papers, and
  so on. Even though I did have to remind students to refer to the
  rubric, I knew that having my evaluative criteria posted from the
  outset provided the students with their best chance for success.
  Spending time up-front on these rubrics prevents misunderstandings about your grading and gives both you and the students something to point to in the event of any dispute. One should, of course,
  have these available in all courses, but in courses where students will
  never have the opportunity to meet with you face-to-face, they are
  especially imperative.
- If you happen to be a night-owl, you will find that being online with
  your class in the late evening is a rewarding experience. It provides
  the sensation that you are "talking" to your students, and they seem
  more relaxed, thinking it's "cool" to have a professor who keeps
  their hours.

- The first time around, know that you're going to experience some inefficiencies in your use of time. You will need an adjustment period between feeling as though you need to check your course site every hour, and resisting the temptation to not check it at all for 24 hours so you won't discover an assignment fiasco, thus ruining your plans for the day or the weekend. Set limits for yourself: try various times of day, and see what works best for you. After one disastrous period where I spent 20 hours online in two days, I reasoned that our face-to-face summer classes met for eight contact hours per week, so I used that as a baseline for how much time I should be spending on the course site. As with a traditional class, of course, time spent evaluating papers, preparing assignments, and formulating discussion questions was extra.

- Let the students know up-front any days when you will *not* be available online. In my caveat, I told students I would not be available Fridays and Saturdays. It turned out that a better guideline (and I revised it to suit my schedule) was that I would not be available Saturday evenings and Sundays. I had to get away from the mindset that class met Mondays through Thursdays for two hours in the summer, or two evenings a week, for four hours each. I tried to make sure I was always available the day before an assignment; consequently, I broke my habit of Monday assignments since I wanted my summer Sundays free. Assignments were usually due on Tuesdays or Thursdays.

- Finally, if having students do collaborative work is important in your discipline, make sure they do it. Surprisingly, some students have never used a *wiki* before, but your course shell most likely has a "Wiki" tool available. When I taught this course face-to-face, I had a class wiki, and students created their own individual wikis for the group project. Because my summer class was so small, I did not use the wiki tool. Before offering your course, be sure you know how to use the wiki tool, so that you can instruct your students to do the same for group work. Be careful how you structure the collaborative assignment, so that you don't get caught in the bind that I did: I was so happy with the way my face-to-face assignment had turned out, I didn't make the necessary adjustments in time to provide an effective online experience.

Different: that's my final word for online courses. Not better than, or worse than, face-to-face classes. Certainly worth doing for what they provide in accessibility for students, and for your own teaching development. Enjoy your steps toward accessibility for all!

REFERENCES

Brennan, K. (2002). *Being with Rachel: a story of memory and survival.* New York: W.W. Norton.

Corker, M., & French, S. (1999). *Disability discourse: Disability, human rights, and society.* Buckingham: Open University Press.

Irvin, C. (2004). *Home bound: Growing up with a disability in America.* Philadelphia, PA: Temple University Press.

Mezey, S. G. (2005). *Disabling interpretations the Americans with Disabilities Act in federal court.* Pittsburgh, PA: University of Pittsburgh Press.

Smith, C. F. (2005). *Writing public policy: a practical guide to communicating in the policy-making process.* New York: Oxford University Press.

Wilson, J. C., & Lewiecki-Wilson, C. (2001). *Embodied rhetorics: disability in language and culture.* Carbondale: Southern Illinois University Press.

CHAPTER 4

TRANSFORMATIVE TEACHING

From Classroom Lectern to Internet-Based Learning Platforms

Adam David Roth

Traditional approaches to teaching and learning are undergoing extensive revision in the age of Internet-based educational technologies. Many recent developments in higher education emphasize the need to incorporate Internet-based technologies into all classes so as to address a new generation of learners who are raised in a technologically advanced society accustomed to learning via the Internet. More recently, many colleges and universities are making distance education—through the Internet—more the norm than the exception by extending program offerings for online degrees and certifications. Certainly, this is a pivotal time when many instructors are faced with the question of whether or not to begin teaching online courses. This chapter addresses the author's initial reservations about teaching online and outlines the decision-making process that guided the conversion of an upper-level Communication Studies course, The Ethics of Persuasion, *from the brick-and-mortar setting of the traditional classroom to the multi-dimensional, online platform of a learning management system. The chapter shows how online courses can be designed in ways that are both consistent with the methods, goals, and philosophies of traditional education while at the same time contributing to and supplementing them in significant ways, thereby promoting student learning and the retention of course material.*

The concept of delivering instruction online is one that is not going to fade away. It is not an educational fad or the latest buzzword used to impress our

Taking Your Course Online: An Interdisciplinary Journey, pages 35–52
Copyright © 2012 by Information Age Publishing
All rights of reproduction in any form reserved.

35

stakeholders. The ivory tower as it was once known has now firmly established itself as a digital one. The change in the ways and means of educating students of higher learning does not need to be viewed in a negative light; however, many faculty are reluctant to move from behind the lectern to a computer screen. This resistance to change is not without merit... teaching online requires a faculty member to think differently about teaching and learning, learn a host of new technological skills and engage in ongoing faculty development for design and development of quality online instruction, and play the role of teacher, learner, and technical support.

—Fish and Wickersham (2009)

When I took part in a semester-long, online-teaching seminar in the Spring of 2009—with the goal of training faculty to develop and teach effective online courses—I was ambivalent, intimidated, and skeptical about teaching online for the very first time. Certainly, I have used technology in my classes before—presentation slides, video cameras, DVDs, and learning management systems; once I was even a Teaching Assistant for a satellite-delivered, distance-education class when I was a graduate student at the University of Iowa. While I am no stranger to technology, I resisted opportunities to pursue online teaching assignments—until recently—for two main reasons: On the one hand, I respected and defended the conventional model of education, where students and teacher meet in the physical space of the classroom, with all of our senses involved in learning; on the other hand, I doubted that internet-based technologies could produce contexts dynamic enough for deep learning to occur, and I was hesitant to invest time trying to find out if they could.

Despite teaching in higher education for only a decade, I feel old-fashioned for privileging the immediacy, intimacy, and dynamics afforded by brick-and-mortar classes, the unique sense of camaraderie that develops in them among students and instructor over the course of the semester, and the learning experiences that we all share in together. I am used to *seeing* students, attending and adapting to each of their ideas, questions, and needs; I am always conscious of their frustrations, preoccupations, and distractions as well as how they gauge and register mine. Coupled with the lively, but contingent, nature of class discussions, the uncertainty we all periodically feel during them and, most of all, the wonderful, many-times laughable, learning experiences they produce, this, to me, is an educational climate conducive to a culture of inquiry. It's also what makes teaching and learning seem real to me, memorable, impressionable, authentic, and somewhat unpredictable.

Notwithstanding my possible idealism, I was distrustful that technology could ever replicate for students and me the community and culture of learning that I have grown accustomed to in my conventional classes. I was equally apprehensive about my own readiness as an online teacher, despite the top-of-the-line training I received from my university's online-teaching experts. What remained to be seen, however, was how *I* would adapt my teaching principles and behaviors to an online "classroom" to meet the needs and expectations of cyber-students, and, in the process, learn, manage, negotiate and exploit the limitations and possibilities of the technology we were using. My main concern in the process of transitioning from face-to-face to Internet-based teaching was that I not relinquish any of the principles and goals that have always made me a successful teacher in the classroom.

Not until *after* participating in the online-teaching faculty-development seminar, and *following* the end of my first (somewhat unsuccessful) semester teaching online, did I begin to fully appreciate and think seriously about the merits of Internet-based education, and to make a place for it within my own philosophy of teaching. This chapter explores the merits I discovered, and the mistakes I made and the lessons I learned in the process of converting an upper level, Communication Studies course, *The Ethics of Persuasion*, from the brick-and-mortar classroom to a purely online platform. The chapter opens with a defense of online teaching, specifically detailing my rationale for making the plunge into the world of online education. Next, the chapter identifies pedagogical principles—drawn from the history of distance education and contemporary instructional theory—that inform the conversion of my *Ethics of Persuasion* course from a traditional, face-to-face class, to a multi-dimensional, online course delivered through a learning management system. The third and final section of the chapter highlights some of the mistakes I made during my first semester teaching online and describes how I revised my online course accordingly, thereby offering useful lessons for instructors to follow who may be considering, or who already are, teaching online. An overarching narrative in the chapter tells how time-honored pedagogical principles—like ones derived from Plato—can guide the effective development of online courses and online-learning communities. I remain skeptical about certain approaches to distance education, but I now teach online courses not just because they are convenient and I can teach them at any time and from any place—which is an obvious added benefit—but because I believe in and defend the Internet as a medium with serious educational potential, although it requires significant investment in time, energy, and thought to be used effectively for distance learning.

MY DEFENSE OF DISTANCE EDUCATION

One of the reasons I am determined to become an online teacher is because I am convinced that Internet-based education is the wave of the future—whether educators like it or not. As Fish and Wickersham (2009) insist, "[t]he concept of delivering instruction online is one that is not going to fade away. It is not an educational fad or the latest buzzword used to impress our stakeholders. The ivory tower as it was once known has now firmly established itself as a digital one" (pp. 282–283). Educators in the modern academy must accept this paradigm shift in higher education, as well as the likelihood that the new generation of instructors today will—at some point in the not too distant future—be required to offer classes online, or at least classes with a significant online component, if they're not already required to do so—as many academic programs do. The traditional, brick-and-mortar-classroom model of education is undergoing major revision in the age of Internet-based learning technologies, and online courses and Internet-based instruction make a great deal of sense to institutions, not least of all because it can be financially rewarding and is more efficient to deliver than traditional classes, which require space planning, utilities, and so on.

More than being merely profitable and efficient, Kleinman (2005) and Falvo & Johnson (2007) show there is also tremendous pedagogical value in Internet-based educational technologies, and for a long time educators have predicted the central role that technology now plays in higher education. For instance, Phipps and Merisotis (1999) of the Institute for Higher Education Policy, reported that "[t]echnology is having, and will continue to have, a profound impact on colleges and universities in America and around the globe. Distance learning, which was once an often poor and unwelcome stepchild within the academic community, is becoming increasingly more visible as a part of the higher education community" (p. 29). Today, I would argue, online teaching and distance education is not only "more visible," but thoroughly engrained into the fabric of institutional curricula, particularly because studies continue to show that Internet-based models of distance education can produce remarkable results in student learning and their retention and engagement of course material. Furthermore, while many students thrive in the context of the traditional classroom, many others, it seems, perform better in online courses—they participate more and score higher on course assessments.

One of the most optimistic and inspiring features of this trend, and one of the more compelling arguments for its continued growth in higher education, is that the Internet makes education more democratic, equitable, accessible, available to larger and larger numbers of people; it offers alternative approaches and platforms for teaching and learning that often benefit particular students more than conventional classroom approaches do. Students today are raised in a technologically advanced society and many of them are accustomed to—sometimes even more comfortable with—learning and communicating through the Internet, and they expect all of our courses to take advantage of the Internet and the learning management platforms that our institutions make available for us to use. From personal experience, it is easy to see how online courses make education cessible to students for whom education has become increasingly sible—the student who needs one more class before she graduates, but is currently living out of town and working full-time; or that single mother, trying to complete her college degree, raise a child, and negotiate a job in the process. I like to remember this ideal of distance education, even if it only applies to a handful of my students.

TRADITIONAL PEDAGOGICAL PRINCIPLES FOR INTERNET-BASED EDUCATION

Upon reviewing the history of distance education, I discovered that the democratic ideal inherent within distance education is not new, and that the demand for distance education was not created by the invention of the Internet, but rather dates back to the introduction and use of the earliest educational technologies. In the fifth- and fourth-century BCE Greece, writing was just being introduced as the innovative communication technology of the day, while the technology of rhetoric—which used oratory and strategies of persuasion for personal, political, and legal gain—was already widely adopted and utilized. As I prepared to teach my first online course, I could not help but reflect on what Plato—the initial adversary of distance education and the educational technologies of rhetoric and writing employed by the Sophists—would say about online teaching. Taking the plunge into the world of online teaching positioned me much like a Greek Sophist, touting technology for educational purposes, defending its legitimacy as an effective learning tool. All the while I could imagine Plato cautioning me about the need for immediacy, intimacy, and interactivity in education, and the dangers involved in teaching only the "appearance of wisdom."

Plato's principles for distance education. By re-reading Plato's dialogues, however, I realize that even Plato, somehow, finds a way to circumvent his own strict criticisms of writing and rhetoric in order to convey philosophical peace-offerings to posterity. As such, Plato supplies some of the first pedagogical principles for the effective use of educational technologies, and he gives me reassurance that distance education can be successful, if it follows a proper "method."

Although many people may assume that the discourse of educational technology is a contemporary one, Plato inaugurated this discourse in ancient Greece by drawing attention to the dangers of rhetoric and writing—the innovative communication technologies of the day. In *Phaedrus*, for example, the dialogue begins with Socrates' meeting and conversation with the young student, Phaedrus. In summary, Phaedrus, who has just run into Socrates, lauds a speech just delivered by his mentor, Lysias. Socrates, confessing to be a lover of discourse and oratory, pleads with Phaedrus to re-cite the speech for him. Phaedrus, feigning shyness, insists that he can't recall the discourse from memory; but Socrates is convinced that Phaedrus has a written copy of the speech hidden under his cloak, and he persuades Phaedrus to reveal and read it. While the topic of the speech and its importance to the framework and intention of the dialogue is subject to much debate, a clear point is that Socrates proposes to deliver a better speech, one that is inspired by the moment—off the cuff. Socrates' intent here is obviously to advertise his better skills as a superior orator, to possibly seduce Phaedrus to leave Lysias and become his student instead.

One of the morals I derive from this summary of the speeches in the dialogue is that written texts—like the speech Lysias writes and Phaedrus re-cites—are poor substitutes for the lively, inspired, present nature of face-to-face dialogue. Socrates criticizes Lysias for using written speeches—as many Sophists did in ancient Greece—to educate students through example. Written discourse, as Plato makes clear in other parts of the dialogue, is physiologically bankrupt; devoid of life; a dead *logos*. Metaphorically, Plato describes writing as a bastard child that stands indefensible in its father's (author's) absence because it is incapable of replying to questions that readers pose (Plato, 2007, p. 275d-e). Unlike face-to-face dialogue and dialectic, writing is impersonal and promiscuous; it is not adapted or personalized to the soul of an individual, but rather can be read by any person who comes into contact with it (Peters, 2001). Lacking vitality and conscious discretion, and with no way of defending itself, the experience of reading and learning from such a dead *logos*, is passive, depersonalized, and inauthentic.

Through the Egyptian myth of Theuth and Thamus, Plato explains how writing is not a tool for teaching or a means to learning, but rather an aid to memory that produces not memory and truth, but "forgetfulness" and the "appearance of wisdom." The legend begins with Theuth delivering to Thamus, the King of Egypt, the art of letters, which he insists "will make the Egyptians wiser and will improve their memories; for it is an elixir of memory and wisdom . . . " (274e). The King is not persuaded and thinks

> . . . this invention will produce forgetfulness in the minds of those who learn to use it, because they will not practice their memory. Their trust in writing, produced by external characters which are no part of themselves, will discourage the use of their own memory within them. You have invented an elixir not of memory, but of reminding; and you offer your pupils the appearance of wisdom, not true wisdom, for they will read many things without instruction and will therefore seem to know many things, when they are for the most part ignorant and hard to get along with, since they are not wise, but only appear wise. (Plato, 2007, p. 275a-c)

Writing is an external aid to memory, not real memory, and it instills in readers the appearance of wisdom and knowledge, but not true knowledge, which can only be obtained from inside us. Compared to the dynamic, interactive, personalized, and engaging nature of the dialectical method of philosophy and learning that Plato advances, writing discourages the use of one's mind and memory.

From *Phaedrus* and Plato's critique of writing and rhetoric, we can discern several general principles about education that are useful in our discussion of online teaching. Plato reminds us that education should be adapted and personalized to the soul of an individual, which requires that an educator promote critical reflection through the interactive and lively engagement and exchange of ideas. Real learning and true knowledge are not produced passively, through reading, or impersonally, through writing. Rather, wisdom is generated through contexts that are characterized by immediacy and intimacy, and that encourage critical reflection on ideas.

The question remains: Why does Plato write dialogues when writing is in clear violation of the Socratic conception of philosophy, with its emphasis on the present, active, lively, give-and-take exchange of ideas characteristic of face-to-face disputation and dialectic? If Plato truly believes that philosophy cannot be fully manifested through writing, then why do his written texts reek of philosophical inquiry? And, if Plato does not fully commit his philosophy to writing, then how should we read and interpret his dialogues today? Answers to these questions allow me to appreciate how Plato comes to terms with the technologies of his day, and how he harnesses their educational potential to provoke critical inquiry and reflection, in much the same way that I now do in my online classes.

Rather than understanding writing as an attempt to re-present Socratic philosophy and principles—which Plato has little faith in writing's ability to do anyway—I argue that writing is an integral part of Plato's conception of philosophy, a way of generating a philosophical relationship between the text and its readers. Plato's written conception of philosophy does not manifest in a representation of dialogical exchanges, but rather in the dramatic effects these exchanges may have on readers. Therefore, I do not interpret Plato's dialogues as gestures aimed at preserving and distributing knowledge through writing, but performatively, as dramatic events aimed at enacting the ongoing process of intellectual inquiry in all of its stages. This performative enactment of inquiry enables readers through the centuries to experience the journey to self-knowledge as though they were themselves part of it.

Plato uses the dialogue form to reconcile, on the one hand, the limitations he perceives in writing and rhetoric, and on the other hand, the possibilities for philosophy to use rhetoric and writing to affect large audiences, especially into the future. The dialogue form, then, enables Plato to mimic—as closely as possible—the dialectical method in action so that readers

rticipants in a dialogue but become actively engagement
ways finding in it new directions and ideas. In this way,
the limitations of writing and rhetoric and, hence, his
em, by avoiding the use of technology as a method for
t, and using it instead as a provocation to further insight
and critical inquiry. As such, Plato leaves an indelible mark on distance education, offering us a model—albeit an ancient one—for engaging students from a distance, developing enticing contexts and discourses that students want to take the initiative to engage in.

Lessons learned from earlier models of distance education. While the Sophists and Plato may be the earliest pioneers of distance education, certainly the initial adopters (and in Plato's case, opponent too) of educational technologies, they are easily forgotten in a long history of distance education that spans the use of many—if not all—communication technologies. In the history of the West, for every new technology that gets adopted for educational purposes, from rhetoric to writing, through the printing press, radio, and the Internet, critics resurface and rehash many of the same arguments that Plato lodged against rhetoric and writing; educational technologies in United States history are no exception.

In the United States, distance education became popular as a way for individuals who could not attend traditional classes—military personnel, farmers, and stay-at-home mothers—to have access to college credits and degrees. The introduction of a reliable and fast mail-delivery service in the nineteenth century allowed the mail-correspondence model of distance education to become widely used. Adams (2006) explains that distance education in the United States began when

> ...the first college-level courses were offered by mail in 1873 when Illinois Wesleyan University developed a curriculum of courses leading to a bachelor's, master's or doctoral degrees (Bittner & Mallory, 1933). In 1870, the Chautauqua Institute started to offer 'unofficial' instruction in French and German by correspondence. It was not until 1883, however, that the State of New York granted a charter to the Chautauqua College of Liberal Arts to award degrees to students completing a curriculum in Sunday School teaching. (pp. 3–4)

By 1890, the University of Chicago, an early pioneer in distance education, included the University Extension as one of its five divisions, through which in 1892 a correspondence program was established to offer instruction—through mail—to remote students. The program started with 39 courses and 82 students, and it grew by 1906 to almost 300 courses and 1600 students (Adams, 2006).

The goal of democratizing learning through distance education was achieved, in part, through the designations of land grant schools. As Aggarwal (2007) explains, "in the United States, the notion of land grant college with a campus extending to the state boundaries led American universities to offer correspondence courses from the 1890s... the concern was to reach students who were isolated from regular institutional teaching and to try to compensate for some of the disadvantages of isolation" (p. 7). In particular, these courses were viewed as an excellent way of providing college-level instruction to people in remote locations, and to women who enrolled in correspondence courses at a much higher rate than males did, most likely because they were primary caretakers at home, and lacked the mobility required to attend live lectures and classes (Dobbs, Waid, & del Carmen, 2009, p. 10).

The early twentieth century experienced an explosion of correspondence-learning programs, and the International Correspondence Schools reported that between 1892 and 1899 enrollments in correspondence programs increased across the country from 10,000 to 80,000. By 1906, astoundingly, enrollments in correspondence courses were reported to have increased ten-fold to 900,000, and rose to more than 2 million students by 1927! By 1920, the University of Chicago, one of the original institutions to offer distance education, was only one of 73 American universities across 39 states that delivered credit programs through distance education on a variety of academic and professional subject matters (Dobbs et al., 2009).

The rise of enrollments in correspondence- and distance-education programs provoked a great deal of criticism from educators and the public alike. In 1926, The National Home Study Council was formed to monitor the practices of correspondence schools after decades of allegations about fraudulent business practices, poor instruction, and the proliferation of diploma mills that negatively affected the image of legitimate correspondence programs.

Despite a steady barrage of criticism, the influx of innovative communication technologies during the early part of the twentieth century increased the demand, and at the same time lessened the burden for delivering remote instruction; radio, movies and television are most responsible for this change. As Saettler (1968) explains:

> In the United States the first catalog of instructional films was published in 1910. Later that year, the public school system of Rochester, New York became the first to adopt films for regular instructional use. In 1913, Thomas Edison proclaimed: "Books will soon be obsolete in the school... It is possible to teach every branch of human knowledge with the motion picture. Our school systems will be completely changed over the next ten years." (p. 98)

While Edison's prediction did not come true, it was prescient of the television- and digital-age to come, and the paradigm shift that would compel higher education to incorporate and adapt to these new educational technologies.

By 1930, televised courses were being developed at the University of Iowa, nine years before television premiered at the World's Fair, and before NBC began a regular broadcasting schedule. Radio courses and lectures, on the other hand, were already being offered, as colleges and universities began applying for and receiving Federal Communications Commission licenses to broadcast over the airwaves. The first educational radio licenses were granted to the University of Salt Lake, the University of Wisconsin, the University of Minnesota, and Pennsylvania State University.

The end of World War II produced an increased demand for distance education as government, industry, and the pubic emphasized the need to prepare and train returning service-people to reenter the national workforce. At this time, television became a commonplace method for delivering instruction to returning veterans, who took advantage of the education entitled to them through the G.I. Bill. Later, in the 1970s and 1980s, color television, cable channels, and the development of the video cassette recorder and videotapes, all afforded students and educators with more possibilities for distance education, possibilities that were more engaging and interactive than earlier technologies had been.

Enrollments in correspondence and distance-education courses actually declined over the middle part of the century for several reasons, including the founding of colleges and universities across the country, making classrooms more physically accessible to students. Another reason was its critics, who insisted—as critics always have—that distance education is a poor substitute for face-to-face learning. Lastly, institutions had a hard time finding instructors to teach distance-education courses, especially if it required teaching and grading papers through the mail (which many of us do anyway with e-mail today!) Not until the introduction of Internet-based distance education (reportedly in 1984 with undergraduate courses being offered online at the New Jersey Institute of Technology) did higher education discover a technology that surmounts many of the limitations and obstacles imposed by earlier models of distance learning (Aggarwal, 2007).

INTERNET-BASED DISTANCE EDUCATION: CONVERTING FROM FACE-TO-FACE TO ONLINE CLASS

More than just a means to credits or a degree, some educators and students argue that Internet-based distance-education programs can be a transformative experience for students who begin to develop—through online learning—the tools and skills that will be required of them as citizens in a technologically advanced society. Fabry (2009) explains that "shifting from traditional to online teaching requires a thoughtful consideration of how best to use a learner-centered approach in the delivery of online instruction to optimize instructor-learner interaction" (p. 254). In this "learner-centered approach," students are charged with more responsibility over their education than they are in traditional classrooms.

> As students begin to assume more responsibility for their own knowledge generation and overall learning experience, they become empowered to continually seek out new information and learning, and collaborate with peers and coworkers in problem solving and solution creations. This disposition is critical in today's technologically advanced society where information and technology change on a daily basis and we become a more global-based society. (Dawley, 2007, p. 4)

Like the readers of Plato's dialogues, students in online courses should be enticed and positioned to actively engage in and produce the discourse of the class, which doubly teaches them life skills for being in the world.

We, as educators, no less than students, have more responsibility in this new age of Internet-based learning, which involves its own learning curve that instructors must ascend if we want to become effective online teachers. Swan (2002) reminds us of what "Coppola et al. (2001) asserted that in any environment, teachers have three roles—cognitive, affective, and managerial . . . online, the cognitive role shifts to one of deeper complexity, the affective role requires faculty to find new tools to express emotion, and the managerial role requires greater attention to detail, more structure, and additional student monitoring" (pp. 25–26).

MISTAKES I MADE AND LESSONS I LEARNED

I wish I had known all of this before making the many mistakes I did during my first semester teaching online, but, in retrospect, what I now know about the history of distance education and what many of its critics have alleged, informs my understanding of these mistakes, and the lessons I've learned to correct them. As optimistic as I may have been about my first online course, the reality is that it was somewhat of a flop, mainly because I was not ready—psychologically—to be an online teacher. My class got off to a good start, and I used many of the immediacy tactics I learned in my training seminar—sending out a welcome letter at the beginning of the semester, explaining course policies and guidelines upfront, and immediately using an introductory discussion assignment to learn more about my students. But I can't say for sure that a true culture and community ever developed in it. Part of that may be because my expectations for "class" participation were unclear, and I had to remind students of their obligation to write in discussion forums and to participate in discussing ideas. The (meta) structure of the course, however, was disorganized and impersonal, and the discussions I provoked never got much better than bland. Although my teaching evaluations were decent, I attributed that to my inability to justify giving low grades, particularly when my expectations in the course were unclear. It was easy to discern from the flood of e-mails I received from students throughout the semester that I had taken too much for granted in my instructions, even though I thought they were entirely clear. Lesson one: instructions for assignments in online classes can never be too clear.

The biggest mistake I made is in the way I envisioned the framework of the course, and this is where Plato comes in handy to correct me. In too many ways, my course was structured around a content-delivery model of instruction, which is not conducive to learning in online courses; it was almost as if I was using my learning management system as a glorified photocopying machine instead of a dynamic platform for engaging and guiding students in a semester-long intellectual inquiry. Like Plato reminds us, and contemporary instructional theorists attest, distance education requires a paradigm shift away from this model of instruction where teacher delivers content and information to students, and more toward an engagement with students and their ideas, whereby students take on part of the responsibility for interactivity, provided that the instructor realizes this as a goal of the course.

It was difficult to come to terms with being an ineffective online teacher because I take great pride in my teaching and the recognition it has received from students and colleagues. In some ways, however, what makes me a good teacher in the classroom is no longer applicable to online environments. For instance, student teaching evaluations have consistently praised my public speaking, and my passion for the subject matter. Unfortunately, my public speaking skills are irrelevant in the Internet-based world of distance education. In online courses, I cannot use my voice to excite and energize students, who then mimic the energy I always attempt to elicit from them, or to verbally probe and question students and to guide them from lower- to higher-order levels of thinking. The online teaching environment requires a completely different educational toolbox. Technically, I could record every one of my lectures on audio or video and upload them to a server—feign authenticity in a medium that easily draws attention to its structural representativeness—but the energy and dynamic nature of the traditional classroom would be absent, and my recorded lectures would be no better than the speeches written by the Sophists, whom Plato attacks.

BUILDING COMMUNITIES OF LEARNING
IN ONLINE ENVIRONMENTS

The foundation for any culture of inquiry is a sense of community, a feeling of intimacy with others, and an acknowledgement of camaraderie. Plato knew this and that's why he insisted on understanding the souls of his students, and adapting discourse accordingly to suit their individual and intellectual needs. To him, education was intimate, even erotic, filled with passion that was directed toward the discovery of universal truths.

Building a sense of community and a culture of inquiry is no less important in online courses. It is hard to identify, however, exactly what it is that I do in the classroom that generates a conducive culture and environment for learning. I am honest, yes; fair, too. I also like to think that I am just with my students, and respectful of their ambitions, possibilities, and limitations. I have found that humor is a prerequisite for both an intimate lecture and classroom setting. The frequent, in-unison laughs my lectures and interactions with students generate allow students to feel part of a relaxing, while at the same time serious, community. I want my students to enjoy attending class, learning new topics, and having a few laughs along the way. Otherwise, it is difficult to pinpoint the development of culture and the dynamics that emerge in my brick-and-mortar classes.

To build a sense of community and a culture of learning in my online *Ethics of Persuasion* course takes a different approach from that required in the traditional classroom. For one, my humor in the classroom does not translate well to my online students, and humor is a large part of what makes for a successful instructor. And, in my online course, I question whether there is ever a *true* community? There is something that takes place in my classroom that cannot be replicated online. What is it? It's the difference between watching a film and seeing a play. There's a vibration; an energy in the air. I am going to sound poetic, but the live classroom experience is breathing, living growth, and a way of seeing the world that involves others—if the live classroom is facilitated properly. It does not have to mean that students engage in a festival of talking . . . it could be everyone listening to a lecture. Still, attention is there and fixed. This is what some students find uncomfortable and stifling about a live classroom—it is so regulated in terms of structure and time; so public. But there is no way to replicate it, however, and the online course falls short.

To make up for it, I make sure my online offering of the *Ethics of Persuasion* is as engaging and interesting as possible, in order to encourage serious engagement with course concepts, and to promote deep learning in my students. As Vess (2005) explains, in online courses, if they are not carefully managed and moderated, emphasis seems to be placed on students and teachers "posting" information, thoughts, and feedback to send to each other. Everyone communicates by writing and could almost be blogging to each other, but who is reading it? Do students truly give it full attention from their homes? Are they listening to the others? Or, are they half-listening, skimming information, maybe even surfing the web simultaneously, and spitting back something to be "read" in the same fashion by the other members of the group. Knowing this is a possibility, I model the goals of my online assignments after the goals Plato sets for his dialogues—to provoke critical reflection and to generate a passionate discourse community, which requires active student engagement, analysis, and reflection.

In my online class, I produce this culture of inquiry by following Plato's advice, remembering to personalize my instruction, to establish a sense of immediacy with my students, to adapt to their souls, and to take the time required to teach to each of them. In the classroom, I do this by engaging all of my students in frequent discussions and in-class writing, pairing, and sharing activities, which generally work well to engender serious and passionate debates. My eyes and body help me to focus my attention where needed, and I like to survey the class with my eyes, and move my focus from student to student, speaking to each of them for a bit of time. Similarly, when it comes time to grading assignments and activities, I like to make my comments personalized—as much as possible given time constraints— because I believe that the personalized element of instruction must never disappear.

In many ways, I am still learning to personalize my online courses, and to do a better job of making sure that my online pedagogy is well-suited and adapted to my cyber-students. In the meantime, however, I make sure to individualize comments and evaluations as much as possible, and insist that students have direct communication with me about paper topic approvals, and about other course checkpoints. Since many of my cyber-students live off-campus, I regularly hold online office hours through the chat room feature of our learning management system, and I encourage students to call my office to discuss readings and assignments.

This open and honest line of communication and the personal bond it produces is one of the goals I set for both my face-to-face and online courses. Particularly in my online course, however, I want to ensure that my students never feel like they are dealing with a remote and impersonal course that is packaged into a learning management system, but rather with an engaging and dynamic professor who is exploiting technology to promote all avenues of learning. Posting a picture of me helps to establish this personal connection with students, and I send out a good, heart-felt welcome letter at the beginning of the semester to enhance and set the tone for the communication climate in the course.

I make sure that my writing in the class serves as a model for the type of writing and communication I expect from my students, and I also develop a clear writing policy at the beginning of the semester that I insist all students follow. Following Plato's model, I ask my students to think seriously about the limitations and possibilities inherent in their writing, and I discourage them from writing recklessly, from blindly replying to other student's posts and passively reading mine. Instead, I attempt to develop a culture of personal writing, where posts are adapted to particular recipients and their ideas, and that allows me to offer individualized feedback and instruction, and prompts toward further inquiry. I make sure students understand how important it will be to be clear and concise in messages, and to write in ways that many readers can understand. At the beginning of my online course, I make sure that our initial discussion assignments are "moderated," which allows me to "deny" and return for revision posts that have misspellings and severe grammatical errors. My experience has been that setting the tone for good writing in the beginning of the semester is essential for ensuring good and promising discussions for the remainder of the term.

CONCLUSION: NOTES ON CONVERTING
FACE-TO-FACE TO ONLINE COURSES

While both teaching in the classroom and teaching online share many of the same goals, the means through which learning is achieved in both is radically different. As this chapter shows, online teaching requires a paradigm shift away from the traditional content-centered model of education to a focus on the instructor as a facilitator of learning in a learner-centered curriculum. In this new paradigm, students have a unique responsibility to take control of their education, and instructors are charged with the difficult task of developing and maintaining intimate, personal, engaging, challenging, yet comfortable, learning environments. The idea that online teaching and online classes are somehow easier than traditional ones is misguided. Online courses, in some ways, require more work than face-to-face classes do, particularly when it comes to displaying immediacy behaviors and facilitating an active, intimate, and engaged community of learning. Like anything else in life, to do it well requires good and proper planning, attention to detail, the ability to adapt to contingency, and the passion to persevere. More than anything else, online teaching demands careful planning upfront, clear execution of assignments and activities, and a level of clarity in directions that mitigates any possibility for confusion.

Distance education is not a new concept, and one can argue that it can be traced all the way back to the Sophists of ancient Greece, who taught by examples and written speeches. Surely in the U.S. distance education has included all forms of media, from lantern slides, to mail-correspondence courses, instructional films, radio and television lectures. The only thing different about online teaching is the medium, its limitations, and its possibilities. To be sure, online teaching will not be the end of the technological pedagogy revolution either. If it began with rhetoric and writing in fifth- and fourth-century BCE Greece, then we can only imagine where technology in education will lead next. Sticking to principles, but adapting to media, I am finding, is also one of my true talents as a teacher—perhaps even better than my knack for public speaking.

More than anything, however, I have learned through teaching online that students can learn well—sometimes even better than in face-to-face classes—through the Internet, so long as the instructor can develop and facilitate a culture and a climate conducive to intellectual inquiry—by asking clear, dynamic, and engaging questions, facilitating learner-centered discussions, and requiring that students play their role in the interactivity that makes online learning work.

Instructors of online courses experience many of the same frustrations that they do in the traditional classroom, except that their approach to addressing these frustrations must be different in the two contexts. For instance, in the classroom it's easy to take a student's partially correct answer and turn it into exactly what you are looking for. In the online class, however, control over discussion is more limited. Who knows when students will read a particular post, and in what order. Therefore, careful attention must be paid to controlling the means of communication among students and instructor, policing and moderating discussions—especially if your learning management system easily allows you to do so with moderated forums and discussions.

Online courses offer educators an extraordinary opportunity to teach students at any time and from any place. They also provide the learner with more opportunities to take advantage of higher education because of the convenience and accessibility of online courses. While this new environment of distance education offers a variety of teaching and learning options that didn't exist even a decade ago, we still need to be highly cognizant of the obstacles and challenges we face as we begin to design and offer online courses.

The requirements and necessary measures to develop and teach online courses are different compared to traditional classes. Good online courses require much more than merely repackaging and rebranding traditional courses, like by uploading presentation slides, assignments, and lecture notes into learning management systems. Many instructors have pointed out—and I tend to agree—that online courses are more difficult and time-consuming to deliver than traditional courses; they require instructors to rethink and restructure how course content is delivered and how learning objectives are set and met (Fish et al., 2009). Making significant adjustments to a course mid-stream will usually confuse students, so develop a course expectations statement for students to read and agree to at the beginning of the term. This document will help students to know what is expected of them and what they can expect from you.

Good and effective online courses should engage students and push them toward higher levels of thinking and encourage a learner-centered approach to education that allows students to play an active role in the development of their transformative learning experiences. On the other hand, successful online courses require strong commitment from individual faculty members, who must display passion and interest for the course, an ability to create online courses that adapt to student needs, provide meaningful examples, motivate students to learn, express and show concern for student learning, and promote immediacy through personalized messages and comments, praise, and so on.

The bottom line about online teaching is that the Internet offers tremendous opportunities for teaching from a distance, but it requires a significant investment of time, careful and detailed planning, clear and engaging assignments, and the ability to adapt to online discussion dynamics and the rate of student learning. Studies have shown reliably that students rate their online courses as highly successful and even personally and educational transformative when they believe that instructors have followed many of the online-teaching best practices that are outlined in this chapter.

REFERENCES

Adams, J. (2006, June 19–23). Lessons learned from the first 50 years of distance education. *International Communication Association*. Dresden, Germany.

Aggarwal, D. D. (2007). *History and scope of distance education*. New Delhi: Sarup & Sons.

Dawley, L. (2007). *The tools for successful online teaching*. London: Information Science Publishing.

Dobbs, R. R., Waid, C. A., & del Carmen, A. (2009). Students' perceptions of online courses: The effect of online course experience. *The Quarterly Review of Distance Education, 10*(1), 9–26.

Fabry, D. L. (2009). Designing online and on-ground course to ensure comparability and consistency in meeting learning outcomes. *The Quarterly Review of Distance Education, 10*(3), 253–261.

Falvo, D. A., & Johnson, B. F. (2007, April). The use of learning management systems in the United States. *TechTrends, 51*(2), 40–45.

Fish, W. W., & Wickersham, L. E. (2009). Best practices for online instructors: Reminders. *The Quarterly Review of Distance Education, 10* (3), 279–284.

Kleinman, S. (2005, January). Strategies for encouraging active learning, interaction, and academic integrity in online courses. *Communication Teacher, 19*(1), 13–18.

Peters, J. D. (2001). *Speaking in the air: A History of the idea of communication*. Chicago: University of Chicago Press.

Phipps, R., & Merisotis, J. (1999). *What's the difference? A review of contemporary research on the effectiveness of distance learning in higher education?* Washington, DC: Institute for Higher Education Policy.

Plato. (2007). *Phaedrus* (1st ed.). Fairfield, IA: 1st World Library, Literary Society.

Saettler, P. (1968). *A history of instructional technology*. New York: McGraw-Hill.

CHAPTER 5

CONVERTING IMMEDIACY TO THE ONLINE CLASSROOM

A Course in Family Communication

Rachel L. DiCioccio

This chapter explains the process of transforming a family communication course from the face-to-face context to the online setting. Specifically, I discuss the role of teacher immediacy by identifying and evaluating the strategies for accomplishing immediacy in the delivery of both versions of the course. Reflecting on the efficacy of particular verbal immediacy techniques, I hope to contribute to the conversation on best practices in online teaching.

As the demand for online undergraduate courses increases, so too does the examination and evaluation of the efficacy of online pedagogy. What are the instructional strategies that impact how we teach and how students learn in the online classroom? Central to answering this question is the issue of teacher immediacy. Researched extensively through the lens of instructional communication, teacher immediacy is integral to understanding pedagogical success. Immediacy has been defined as a set of communication behaviors that influence perceptions of physical and psychological closeness (Mehrabian, 1969; Richmond, Gorham, & McCroskey, 1987).

Taking Your Course Online: An Interdisciplinary Journey, pages 53–65
Copyright © 2012 by Information Age Publishing
All rights of reproduction in any form reserved.

These behaviors include both nonverbal and verbal strategies that "signal accessibility, involvement, arousal, and interest" (Andersen, Nussbaum, Pecchioni, & Grant, 1999, p. 371). How do we go about translating these recognized behaviors from the traditional face-to-face classroom to the online setting?

This chapter will help to illuminate this transformation through the broader discussion of converting a course on family communication. In the pages that follow, I review the immediacy literature that examines both face-to-face and online instruction. I identify and discuss the structure of the face-to-face delivery of the course and explain the process of transitioning to the online format. Specifically, I address the strategies for establishing immediacy in both instructional settings. Finally, I consider the efficacy and success of these techniques in circumventing the obstacles to immediacy presented by online teaching.

IMMEDIACY

Teacher immediacy has been studied in relation to individual variables like teacher competence and character (Frymier & Thompson, 1992) and student affect for teacher (McCroskey, Richmond, Sallinen, Fayer, & Barraclough, 1995). Teacher immediacy has also been associated with learning outcomes such as motivation to study (Christophel, 1990; Christophel & Gorham, 1995; Frymier, 1994), affective learning (Andersen, 1979; McCroskey et al., 1995; Witt, Wheeless, & Allen, 2004), and cognitive learning (Rodriguez, Plax, & Kearney, 1996). Overall, research underscores the relationship between highly immediate teachers and positive instructional outcomes.

Research consistently suggests that if teachers minimize the perceived psychological distance between themselves and their students, they will significantly impact the degree of student learning. The goal of immediacy is to establish a relationship and sense of connection between the instructor and students that will serve to foster interest in course content and strengthen students' commitment to accomplishing course goals (Allen, Witt, & Wheeless, 2006). A variety of behaviors constitute immediate communication. Nonverbally, we can employ eye contact, smiling, head nods, and gesturing to bridge the distance between teacher and student. Leaning toward a person or stepping out from behind the podium also helps to increase relational closeness. Gorham (1988) identified verbal immediacy behaviors such as inclusive talk, using first names, asking questions, and sharing personal examples as equally useful strategies.

Constant and regular use of both nonverbal and verbal immediacy behaviors is more likely to result in greater student appreciation for the teacher and the course. Immediate teachers are more successful at encouraging students to set and achieve positive learning outcomes (Frymier, 1994). According to Christophel (1990), immediacy helps to fuel students' motivation to learn and excel. Once motivated, students have a much better chance of performing beyond the average expectations of the course. In this way teacher immediacy sparks a drive and determination that might not otherwise develop through course content alone. Another view of immediacy focuses on the affective model of learning. Student affect reflects the positive attitude toward the instructor, the subject matter, and the learning experience that is created through the teacher's use of immediacy (Rodriguez et al., 1996). This suggests that when students enjoy the learning experience, they are more willing to participate, which consequently improves their ability and performance in the course.

Research on teacher immediacy is not limited to face-to-face interaction. A growing body of literature examines the use of teacher immediacy in the virtual classroom. The computer-mediated and asynchronous nature of online instruction poses some distinct obstacles to engaging in immediacy. Delayed feedback, a lack of nonverbal channels, and a potentially limited social presence all challenge the means through which immediacy is accomplished. Even with these inherent barriers, however, research findings demonstrate that immediacy can be successfully conveyed in the online classroom (LaRose & Whitten, 2000; O'Sullivan, Hunt, & Lippert, 2004).

Although the majority of online courses do not allow for video conferencing—hence eliminating the opportunity for nonverbal immediacy cues—immediacy can still be successfully established through verbal messages alone (Russo & Benson, 2005). In an ethnographic study of three online courses, LaRose and Whitten (2000) identified "frequent give and take between instructors and learners, addressing students by name, immediate feedback on student responses, and sharing personal anecdotes" (p. 323) as useful strategies that establish psychological closeness in the online medium. When examining student perceptions of teachers' immediacy, Freitas, Myers, and Avtgis (1998) found no significant differences in student reports of the quantity and quality of teacher verbal immediacy behaviors for face-to-face or web based courses. This suggests that the efficacy of verbal immediacy cues is not based on the specific medium, but rather, on instructor use of, and skill, in verbal immediacy.

Because online courses potentially can create an isolated and impersonal environment for students, verbal immediacy is essential to develop and promote positive teacher/student and student/student relationships (Russo & Benson, 2005). According to Gunter (2007), "instructors can enhance student satisfaction and achievement in an online course by creating a sense of community" (p. 197). Teachers' verbal immediacy can be a valuable tool that contributes to building a sense of community and belonging, and establishes a social network online. Using strategies that help students feel connected to the instructor, the course, and each other strengthens participation and commitment to the learning goals of the course. In a study examining motivation, cognitive learning, and retention in the online context, Gunter (2007) identified strategies like relaying frequent and personalized correspondence, providing regular feedback and recognition, and using emoticons as simple approaches to increasing teacher immediacy and, in turn, student success. Teacher immediacy also contributes to establishing a student-centered—rather than a teacher-centered—learning experience. Incorporating open, student-driven discussion and collaborative problem-solving reinforces the relationship between teacher and student, and works to initiate productive relationships among students (Woods & Baker, 2004).

Collectively, these findings highlight not only the value of using verbal immediacy in online instruction, but the need for thoughtful course design that encourages and fosters such strategies. As Danchak (2002) states, "successful instructors carry out these pedagogical roles in face-to-face classes often subconsciously . . . However, working online requires that we be consciously aware of these roles and have the tools to help us carry out those roles" (p. 1). Thus, in the next section I discuss the design of the face-to-face and online version of a Family Communication course and identify and evaluate the strategies for accomplishing teacher immediacy.

STRUCTURE AND DESIGN OF A FAMILY COMMUNICATION COURSE

Extending from the interpersonal communication context, family communication represents one of the fastest growing bodies of research and areas of study in the discipline. Family communication defines a significant aspect of the communication field that is recognized and offered by the majority of communication departments across the country. My course is designed to familiarize students with the study of communication in the context of family relationships. Utilizing a systems theory perspective, in this course the learner examines the primary and secondary family functions of individual relationships and the family as a whole. The course introduces students to primary and secondary functions such as cohesion, adaptability, themes, images, and boundaries. Learners also scrutinize family aspects like patterns, rules, roles, and narratives. Individual relationship qualities and contexts, including intimacy, stress, forgiveness and parent/child and spousal relationships, are also explored. Finally, students address family processes such as decision-making and crisis resolution. The main text that is used in this course is *Family Communication: Cohesion and Change* by Galvin, Bylund, and Brommel (2008). Several topics are enhanced by supplemental readings from *Family Communication* by Segrin and Flora (2005).

The three credit course is an upper-level undergraduate elective for communication majors. Students are eligible to take the course after successful completion of a sophomore-level interpersonal communication course. The pre-requisite course introduces students to the necessary theoretical foundation of interpersonal communication that prepares students for a more concentrated focus on family communication at the advanced level.

The goal of the course is to help students recognize the complexity of family communication and better understand how the central concepts that define family relationships are reflective of their own family systems. To that end, four central learning outcomes represent the cognitive learning goals for the course. The expectation is that at the end of the course students will: (1) have greater knowledge of family theory and research, (2) understand the unique and complex qualities of family communication, (3) be able to clearly articulate how family communication theory applies to, and is demonstrated in, real-world families, and (4) be able to analyze the situations and experiences of their own family system. These learning expectations serve as the foundation for the structure and course design of both the face-to-face and online versions of the course.

THE FACE-TO-FACE COURSE

Format and assignments. The face-to-face version of the family communication course spans 15 weeks and is delivered twice a week for a period of 75 minutes. The format of the course reflects an active delivery that includes lecture and discussion. Lecture is used as a way to examine and review the central concepts of a particular content area that have been introduced by the readings. The lecture serves as the foundation for the teacher-prompted discussion that emerges. Students are encouraged to not only answer questions posed by the teacher, but also raise their own questions and answer fellow students' questions. The discussion around a given topic allows for a more in-depth dissection of the concepts, while also demonstrating the application value of family communication theory. Rather than creating hypothetical examples, students are asked to contribute their own family experiences or reference a familiar TV family example as the basis for class discussions and as a means of assessing whether the learner has mastered the family communication theory/principle at a level that s/he can apply it practically. I initiate this process by volunteering my own family examples as a starting point for the group to analyze and evaluate. These discussions are guided by several fundamental principles: shared family examples must be pertinent and appropriate, comments and discussion must be theory driven rather than personal, and we must recognize that the value of sharing lies in the diversity of our family experiences. This format is utilized throughout the semester to provide students practice and experience in guiding the class discussions, in order to prepare them for a final graded discussion assignment.

There are three major types of assignments in the face-to-face course. Student learning is in part assessed through two examinations. A midterm exam uses a combination of objective and short answer questions to test students' knowledge on the material covered in the first half of the course. The second, final exam is a take-home final that consists of four broad essays that each integrate several of the theories and perspectives discussed in the course. It is an opportunity for students to demonstrate their ability to apply theory in explaining the relationships between family concepts.

Throughout the semester, students' mastery of course material is also assessed using five, three to four page papers. Each paper centers on a broad question that requires students to draw on theory to substantiate an argument. Rather than writing the "correct" answer, students must justify their explanation through the integration of concepts and the application of theory. The papers are evaluated based on how students articulate their argument, the theory and concepts they choose to support their claims, and their ability to write in a concise and focused manner.

The final assessment component focuses on the students' ability to participate in and lead one class discussion. The group discussion topics center on three areas, parent/child relationships, sibling relationships, and family stress and are initiated by a teacher-prompted question. For example, when covering the topic of family stress, one group of leaders is given the following question:

> Families in the United States are especially vulnerable to unpredictable stress because of the pressure society places on them to be a "lifeboat" in times of crisis. Unpredictable stress can greatly affect the family system. How do families maintain stability during periods of family stress? Do media portrayals of "families in crisis" accurately model coping strategies or do they set unrealistic expectations? How?

For each discussion topic, seven to ten students are assigned the leader role and are responsible for guiding the class as they work to answer the question and unpack the particular issue. Although the entire class has read the material, it is the leaders' responsibility to create a valuable class discussion. Using the question as a departure point, the discussion leaders are expected to develop their argument or position, create examples to demonstrate their point, and generate questions to engage the class in order to adequately address the family communication issue. Student leaders are graded based on their use of theory and examples to produce a productive dialogue and their efforts to draw conclusions around the views and opinions of the other students. The exams, short papers, and discussion groups serve as the evaluation tools that assess students' knowledge and understanding of family theory, as well as their writing and speaking skills.

Accomplishing immediacy. Immediacy is a key component of instructional success. I use both nonverbal and verbal immediacy strategies in the face-to-face version of the family communication course to establish and maintain a positive working relationship with my students. I consciously and actively employ immediacy behaviors throughout the semester as a useful mechanism for building rapport and engaging the class.

Nonverbally, I demonstrate immediacy through consistent eye contact, animated delivery, and close physical proximity. Maintaining eye contact with students is not only a way to hold their attention during a lecture, but a way of connecting interpersonally (Christophel & Gorham, 1995). An animated delivery also helps to sustain interest. More importantly, however, conveying one's enthusiasm for the material through more demonstrative gestures, vocalic, and facial expressions models for the students the very passion and curiosity for the material we are working to spark in them. Finally, immediacy is strengthened by stepping out from behind the podium when teaching the class. The goal is for students to feel like active participants rather than passive receivers of the lecture material. Standing inside a student circle or without any barriers between the teacher and the learners underscores this sense of community engagement.

Verbally, my immediacy behaviors are equally as purposeful. From the beginning of the course, I strategically use verbal messages to increase perceptions of psychological closeness with my students. Learning and using students' names early on in the semester shows recognition and respect, and helps students feel more comfortable in the learning environment. Using inclusionary language such as "we" and "our" is another verbal immediacy strategy that strengthens the connection between teacher and student. Instead of telling students what is going on in their world, we discuss what we are all experiencing. The most significant verbal immediacy behavior I use encourages reciprocal sharing of family experiences. As stated earlier, I offer my own family stories or examples, when appropriate, as a way of demonstrating the communication concepts. Revealing personal information reminds students that instructors are actually living what are often abstract concepts: the instructor and material are part of the real world. Telling our own stories, anecdotes, and experiences helps to foster trust, and in turn increases closeness in the teacher/student relationship. When students feel that they are trusted and are a valuable part of the interaction and relationship, they are more likely to reveal and share their own experiences and ideas.

THE ONLINE COURSE

Format and assignments. Transforming the face-to-face version of the family communication course to an asynchronous format required the redesign of both the delivery method and assessment tools that are used. Although the learning objectives and material remain the same, the approach to accomplishing them is quite different. The delivery of the online version of this course is organized around six central content units that are examined over a 10-week summer session. The six focus areas include: family theories, family functions, family roles and types, family stories, family relationships, and family development and stress. The units consist of several components that constitute the students' class experience. Each unit is identified by a discussion board focusing on a particular content area. The discussion board correlates to the appropriate sections of the text and readings. Each of the six units also includes a presentation that outlines the content as well as video lectures, interviews, or news clips that supplement the subtopics within the content area.

The unit discussion boards are guided by one or two broad questions that I post and require students to integrate theory and examples to successfully demonstrate their knowledge and understanding of the material. For example, in the first unit—family theories—students are asked to respond to the following prompts:

> (1) Argue in favor of utilizing a systems theory perspective to understand family communication. How does it help illuminate the communication process? What might detractors of this perspective say? Be specific in your explanations. (2) Dialectical theory helps us understand the relationship between opposing forces that exist in the family. How do these contradictions reflect the conflict between individual and collective family needs? Address tensions specifically and use examples from your own family to clarify.

To ensure that discussions are productive, valuable, and respectful for all learners, students are expected to enforce the following posting guidelines: (1) all postings should use correct English and proper punctuation and occur on time, (2) responses must answer the question fully, (3) responses must specifically reference unit readings, lectures, movies, and so on, and (4) responses must always be respectful of other participants and topics.

The discussion boards represent the central mechanism for assessing student learning. In order to ensure that students participate and contribute to the dialogue, they also represent one set of graded assignments that contribute to students' final grade in the course. Successful participation in the discussions requires that students not only read the material, but critically consider how concepts are demonstrated in real families. Evaluation of learners' contributions is based on the original ideas asserted in students' posts as well as their responses to, and questions of, fellow students' posts. Students' original posts are evaluated in terms of how well they articulate the particular theories and concepts, how appropriate and useful their application is, and how unique and forward thinking their claim is. An excellent original post is one that answers the question in its entirety through the use of specific examples and references to the readings. Posts should be creative and reflect the interest and curiosity of the student rather than regurgitate the text. Finally, posts must be completed by the deadline in order to earn full credit.

Students' responses to their classmates' posts is the second requirement of the discussion boards. Learners are expected to reflect on what the rest of the class has posted and respond in a thoughtful way. Response posts are evaluated based on how learners further the discussion of the topic by questioning, challenging, or evaluating others' claims. Excellent responses demonstrate students' efforts to engage the class in conversation on the topic. Rather than just saying "nice post" or "I agree," strong responses present something of value to the rest of the class by building on what others have contributed and continuing an interesting dialogue.

The other two assessment components are consistent with the face-to-face version of the course. Students are expected to write four three to four page argument papers that reflect their understanding and application of the reading, and are given a comprehensive final essay exam at the end of the semester.

Accomplishing immediacy. As the literature suggests (Danchak, 2002; Freitas et al., 1998; LaRose & Whitten, 2000), although the online format poses a challenge to immediacy, it is still a viable and useful tool that influences students' experience and understanding in the course. Consistent with my face-to-face course, I approach the use of verbal immediacy in the asynchronous context with a set of purposeful strategies that I believe will help foster a positive relationship with the students and create a sense of community for the class.

Verbal immediacy in the online family communication course is accomplished in three ways. At the start of the course, students are instructed to practice using the discussion boards by introducing themselves, identifying their interest in family communication, and revealing the characteristics that define their family based on the material presented in the first chapter of the text. Although this discussion is not graded, students are asked to go beyond their original post and respond and comment on the posts of their classmates. I initiate this discussion by revealing my own family qualities, relationships, and situations as a way of sharing my interest in studying family communication. The information is, of course, appropriate for the student/teacher relationship; however, it is also personal, detailed, and honest. I want to pique students' interest in me as an instructor and member of a family system, as well as the course. My response is posted before students engage in the discussion themselves. By posting my information before the discussion is started, I have a chance to model for the students the kind of post I am expecting. I respond to every student's introduction post and always pose a question to underscore my interest in their personal information and create a dialogue. This is one way to open the lines of communication and begin to build an interpersonal relationship with the students.

A second immediacy technique is to personalize the feedback that I provide on all of the assignments. I make a point of referencing past posts or conversations that have taken place in an open forum or in a one-on-one exchange. I want students to feel recognized and important to the success of the class. Reminding the learners that I am thinking about their disclosure and contributions since the start of the class, rather than as single statements on a discussion board, helps promote feelings of inclusion and belonging. Lastly, I frequently give public praise and recognition for ambitious and good work. The goal of this strategy is to encourage and motivate students to create high-quality work but, more importantly, to cultivate an awareness of community. I want students to be committed to the course in part because they feel appreciated by the instructor and their classmates.

EVALUATING IMMEDIACY IN THE ONLINE COURSE

Teacher immediacy is a pedagogical practice that helps to foster student success and promote a positive learning environment. Implementing immediacy strategies is a valuable practice for instructors of both face-to-face and online courses. Although the payoff of such strategies may be more easily recognized in the context of the face-to-face classroom, the impact of a teachers' verbal immediacy behaviors in the online setting can also result in significant benefits. In the process of transforming a family communication course to the online medium, I made a concerted effort to integrate verbal immediacy techniques that enhanced my rapport with the students and compensated for the obstacles posed by the asynchronous nature of the course. I consistently employed three tactics focused on increasing perceptions of immediacy: (1) revealing and discussing my personal family story, (2) providing personalized feedback, and (3) offering public recognition. In the next section I review each approach and consider how they impacted the class discussions and the dynamic of the course.

I used the first discussion board as an opportunity to introduce myself to the students, allowing me to simultaneously model my discussion expectations and initiate a rapport. I provided the first posted response to the following question:

Introduce yourself and your family to the rest of the class. What category identified in the text best describes your family and why? You may belong to more
than one! What do you think about the definition of family that the authors
of the text have chosen? How does it apply to your family? Would you change
it in any way?

Students were asked to answer the question and informed that "although it
is not a graded discussion, it will serve to establish our interaction over the
next 10 weeks." My post answered the question with a significant amount
of detail regarding my own family; disclosing its members, our ethnic and
religious heritage, and our feelings toward each other and the family as a
whole. The goal was to encourage students to reflect on their own families
and provide equally substantial information.

Subsequently, I used the information provided in their introduction post
to draw connections between both myself and the student and the student
and the rest of the class. Asking questions about a student's family prompted
them to ask questions about mine, as well as their fellow classmates' families.
Although the majority of the students responded to this immediacy tactic,
I believe that it could have stimulated greater interaction and connection
if I had made it a central piece of future discussions. For example, in later discussions, asking students to reference and relate the information we
learned about each other's families would have produced more meaningful
exchanges and further strengthened the cohesion of the class.

A second verbal immediacy strategy that I used was to provide personalized feedback and evaluation. In the face-to-face classroom we often have
an opportunity to engage in conversations that allow us to regulate student
behavior, elaborate on our evaluations of student work, or clarify our view
of student performance. These functions are usually carried out before or
after class—through casual conversation and interaction —and help students to position themselves in an advisee/advisor relationship with the
instructor. The asynchronous format of the online venue, however, does
not readily allow for this type of interaction to emerge. To compensate
and encourage more in depth communication with my students, I made a
point of referencing past posts and discussion contributions when evaluating their current work. The objective was to reinforce our connection by
recognizing their contributions to the overall progress of the course. Reminding students that I knew who they were as individuals rather than just
graded comments on a specific discussion board affirmed our relationship
and strengthened their commitment to the course.

The third verbal immediacy device I employed was to offer students public praise for quality contributions. The online context can foster feelings of
isolation and separation from the group (Russo & Benson, 2005). Regularly
recognizing students' notable, interesting, and unique input enabled me to
encourage and endorse a sense of community. Beyond being appreciative

of the acknowledgment, students often replicated this behavior by reflecting on how the comments of other classmates enhanced their understanding of the concepts. What started out as a teacher-prompted strategy quickly developed into a frequently used student mechanism for giving credit, showing appreciation, and maintaining respect.

CONCLUSIONS

Overall, my focused and active use of verbal immediacy in the online family communication course proved to be a valuable and challenging undertaking. Identifying face-to-face immediacy strategies and translating them so they can work within the confines of asynchronous interaction, is not only plausible but advantageous. It is a worthwhile pedagogical endeavor that elevates student achievement, instructor effectiveness, and course success.

REFERENCES

Allen, M., Witt, P. L., & Wheeless, L. R. (2006). The role of teacher immediacy as a motivational factor in student learning: Using meta-analysis to test a causal model. *Communication Education, 55,* 21–31.

Andersen, J. F. (1979). Teacher immediacy as a predictor of teaching effectiveness. In D. Nimmo (Ed.), *Communication Yearbook 3* (pp. 543–559). New Brunswick, NJ: Transaction Books.

Andersen, J., Nussbaum, J., Pecchioni, L., & Grant, J. A. (1999). Interaction skills in instructional settings. In A. L. Vangelisti, J. A. Daly, & G. W. Friedrich (Eds.), *Teaching communication: Theory, research, and methods* (pp. 359–374). Mahwah, NJ: Lawrence Erlbaum Associates.

Christophel, D. (1990). The relationships among teacher immediacy behaviors, student motivation, and learning. *Communication Education, 39,* 323–340.

Christophel, D., & Gorham, J. (1995). A test-retest analysis of student motivation, teacher immediacy, and perceived source of motivation and demotivation in college classes. *Communication Education, 44,* 292–306.

Danchak, M. M. (2002). Bringing affective behavior to e-learning. *The Technology Source Archives.* Retrieved April 30, 2010, from http://www.technologysource.org

Freitas, F. A., Myers, S. A., & Avtgis, T. A. (1998). Student perceptions of instructor immediacy in conventional and distributed learning classrooms. *Communication Education, 47,* 366–373.

Frymier, A. B. (1994). A model of immediacy in the classroom, *Communication Quarterly, 42,* 133–144.

Frymier, A. B., & Thompson, C. A. (1992). Perceived teacher affinity seeking in relation to perceived teacher credibility. *Communication Education, 41,* 388–399.

Gorham, J. (1988). The relationship between verbal teacher immediacy behaviors and student learning. *Communication Education, 37,* 40–53.

Gunter, G. A. (2007). The effects of the impact of instructional immediacy on cognition and learning in online classes. *International Journal of Social Sciences, 2,* 196–202.

LaRose, R., & Whitten, P. (2000). Re-thinking instructional immediacy for web courses: A social cognitive exploration. *Communication Education, 49,* 320–338.

McCroskey, J. C., Richmond, V. P., Sallinen, A., Fayer, J. M., & Barraclough R. A. (1995). A cross-cultural and multi-behavioral analysis of the relationship between nonverbal immediacy and teacher evaluation. *Communication Education, 44,* 281–291.

Mehrabian, A. (1969). Some referents and measures of nonverbal behavior. *Behavioral Research Methods and Instrumentation, 1,* 203–207.

O'Sullivan, P. B., Hunt, S. K., & Lippert, L. R. (2004). Mediated Immediacy: A language of affiliation in a technological age. *Journal of Language & Social Psychology, 23,* 464–490.

Richmond, V.P., Gorham, J., & McCroskey, J. C. (1987). The relationship between selected immediacy behaviors and cognitive learning. In M. L. McLaughlin (Ed.), *Communication Yearbook 10* (pp. 574–590). Newburry Park, CA: Sage.

Rodriguez, J. I., Plax, T. G., & Kearney, P. (1996). Clarifying the relationship between teacher nonverbal immediacy and student cognitive learning: Affective learning as the central causal mediator. *Communication Education, 45,* 293–305.

Russo, T., & Benson, S. (2005). Learning with invisible others: Perceptions of online presence and their relationship to cognitive and affective learning. *Educational Technology & Society, 8,* 54–62.

Witt, P. L., Wheeless, L. R., & Allen, M. (2004). A meta-analytical review of the relationship between teacher immediacy and student learning. *Communication Monographs, 72,* 184–217.

Woods, R. H., & Baker, J. D. (2004). Interaction and immediacy in online learning. *The International Review of Research in Open and Distance Learning, 5*(2). Retrieved April 30, 2010, from http://www.irrodl.org/index.php/irrodl/article/view/186/801

SECTION II

SCIENCE AND MATHEMATICS

CHAPTER 6

TEACHING SOCIOLOGY ONLINE

Some Experiences, Problems, and Proposed Solutions

Barbara J. Costello

In summer of 2009 I taught my first fully online course, a 200-level sociology course titled Crime and Delinquency. *I begin this chapter by describing my course and over-all teaching approach to provide some context for what follows. I then discuss some of the difficulties I experienced with my first online teaching experience and in subsequent semesters teaching the same course. I also describe the solutions I've developed for some of those problems, and several things I'm planning to try in the future. One thing is certain, however—teaching online is much more difficult than teaching face-to-face, and I expect my list of problems (and hopefully, solutions) to grow as I continue to develop my online course.*

MY APPROACH TO TEACHING *CRIME AND DELINQUENCY*

The *Crime and Delinquency* course fulfills a social science general education requirement at the University of Rhode Island and is a required course for sociology majors in our Criminology and Criminal Justice program. There is a lot of demand for this course, and sections routinely fill very quickly

Taking Your Course Online: An Interdisciplinary Journey, pages 69–77
Copyright © 2012 by Information Age Publishing
All rights of reproduction in any form reserved.
69

during the regular semester, with enrollment capped at 35 students per section. By contrast, summer session courses are not very popular on this campus, and I have had the course cancelled several times I have attempted to offer it during the summer due to low enrollment. This was one of my motivations for taking the course online—there is huge demand for online courses during the summer, and my course filled very quickly, with a maximum enrollment of 20 students, in the summer session in 2009 and 2010, and during the Spring 2010 semester.

As with all of my classes, my main goal in the *Crime and Delinquency* course is to help students develop their critical thinking skills. In the context of this course, I want my students to achieve two major goals: (1) to be able to understand and evaluate different types of criminological data, and to use these data to answer questions and solve problems relating to the causes of crime and delinquency, and (2) to understand various theoretical explanations of crime and to be able to apply and evaluate them using both qualitative and quantitative data.

I don't use a standard criminology textbook in my course, in large part because I think the encyclopedic approach that most standard texts take is not useful in teaching critical thinking. Instead, I use two short monographs: *Crime and Everyday Life* by Marcus Felson and Rachel Boba (2010), and *Armed Robbers in Action* by Wright and Decker (1997); several short readings covering theories of crime that I supplement with lectures; and, to teach students about crime statistics, I use my own material in addition to publicly-available data on crime such as that available in the *Sourcebook of Criminal Justice Statistics* (Bureau of Justice Statistics, 2010).

A typical class meeting in a face-to-face course might consist of a reading quiz, a 20-minute lecture on the material covered in the reading, and an in-class small group assignment asking students to apply the material to some problem, often an analysis of a current event from the perspective of the author whose work students have read for the class meeting. Students' grades are calculated as follows: 20% of their grade is dependent on their open-notes reading quizzes, 15% on in-class assignments, 20% on two papers, and a total of 45% from three exams, including a final exam.

THE TRANSFORMATION TO ONLINE

My goal in transforming the course to online was to keep as much of the material and assignments the same as they are in the face-to-face course. Obviously, in an online course the assignments, quizzes, and exams are all open-book, which requires some adaptation. In the face-to-face course, I give unannounced reading quizzes during which students are free to use notes they've taken from the readings. I've found that this is successful in getting most students to complete the assigned reading most of the time, and the intermittent nature of the quizzes and their brevity (usually just one short essay question) make grading them a quick task. These kinds of questions are not well-suited to an open-book quiz, however, because students can find the appropriate section of the reading and only read that section to answer the question. I considered using timed quizzes in the online course, as they would essentially prevent this "find the answer" approach. However, in one experimental attempt at a timed quiz, I found that some students still tried to get by without reading the chapter prior to taking the quiz, and I was getting some complaints from students that the ten minutes I had allotted for the question were not enough.

To replace the reading quizzes, then, I decided to give students written assignments on each reading that they would complete individually and submit prior to the beginning of an associated online discussion. The online discussions replace the small group problem-solving assignments I typically use in the classroom, and they provide an opportunity for students to master and apply the material covered in their readings. Because students in the online course are required to write a short paper for every assigned reading, I omitted the paper assignments that I usually used in the face-to-face class and incorporated that content into their regular papers and discussions. The essay exams I give in my face-to-face course emphasize analysis rather than recall, and I often provide students with the questions ahead of time. Thus, I didn't need to make significant changes to my exams. Grades in the online course are calculated as follows: 30% for written assignments, 30% for discussions associated with each assignment, and 40% for three exams, including the final exam.

One of the key changes I needed to make to the course was to add material to the online course that would replace lectures. This was particularly important with regard to my lectures on theories of crime, as I typically do not assign a great deal of reading on crime theories in this introductory level class, and instead rely pretty heavily on lectures. To compensate for this, I started assigning several chapters from *Vold's Theoretical Criminology* (Bernard, Snipes, & Gerould, 2010) to introduce the major theories of crime. This has met with mixed success—some students have trouble getting the most from their reading in this book, which is geared more toward an advanced undergraduate audience than to students in an introductory course. Although many of my students in the online course are advanced undergraduates, I continue to find that many students do not have very good reading comprehension, a problem I discuss further below.

SOME PROBLEMS—AND SUGGESTED SOLUTIONS

Problem One: Students with poor reading comprehension. The biggest problem I've faced with online teaching is that some students have poor reading comprehension, which affects every aspect of their learning in an online course. Not only do they not get as much as they should from the readings, but they also seem to have trouble understanding instructions for assignments and written feedback from me. Although part of the problem is doubtless the result of students not taking the time to read carefully, I'm convinced that a small percentage of students don't have good enough reading comprehension to make online courses the best choice for them.

For example, students in the online course are assigned to read Chapter 1, "Fallacies of Crime" in Felson and Boba (2010). In this chapter, the authors outline ten ideas about crime that they argue are fallacious. For part of students' written assignment for this reading, I provide them with a newspaper article or opinion piece that commits one or more of the fallacies, asking students to identify the fallacies committed in the article and explain their answers. Both times I've used this assignment I've had several students (probably 15% of the students in my class) actually commit the fallacy in their answers. Based on comments I've gotten from some of these students when they receive failing grades on assignments like this one, some of them also do not know that they have poor reading comprehension.

Another example is the "failing assignment." In this instance, it was clear to me that the student made some effort at reading a short, two-page reading assignment, but it was also clear that she really didn't understand it. This student was shocked to receive a failing grade on the assignment, and asked me for additional feedback. She sent me the following e-mail message:

> You said that I should take a look at your comments to see where I went wrong. The comments you left on assignment 3 simply stated I was wrong and instructed me to re-read the reading. Something isn't making sense in the reading if I'm not doing well with the homework. It's not that I am avoiding the questions you're asking in the assignments, I think the problem is I don't fully understand what is going on. This material is new to me, so reading it and trying to teach it to myself without any guidance from someone who is familiar with it is not easy. In other online classes I've taken, the professors post notes or use Power Points to help the students better understand the material. I know you posted something for causation and correlation, and I tried to use it when I completed that assignment, but I still wasn't clear on that concept. The readings in Volt are difficult. In my opinion, it is a lot harder to read and understand than Felson and Boba.

Solutions to Problem One. In my syllabus I provide a list of suggestions for students to help them get the most out of their readings, such as "get the big picture of the reading," "ask what the title, headings, and subheadings mean," and "think about what the author is doing in addition to what s/he is saying; for example, is the author presenting his or her own ideas, or those of another? Does s/he agree or disagree with the other author's ideas?" These suggestions don't seem to be enough for some students, if they're reading them at all (see the discussion below on repetition of instructions.)

Another solution I've tried is to provide some very basic reading questions specific to each required reading. Because most of my assignments require application rather than simple description of the reading, some students may find it easy to overlook the fact that basic understanding is required before application or analysis can be done effectively. For example, when I assign the reading on fallacies of crime, I ask students to first provide a definition of the term "fallacy" to help them see the main point of the chapter. Although I still have some students make mistakes with this concept in their assignments and discussion, it does seem to help students focus on the big picture of the chapter and understand that the chapter is a critique of commonly accepted ideas about crime. Additionally, very useful assignments to help students improve their reading comprehension are discussed in Erickson, Peters, and Strommer (2006).

With regard to feedback on assignments, I also plan to provide students with more examples of good and bad assignments, exams, and discussion postings to give them a better sense of what they should be trying to achieve with their writing. I occasionally do this in both online and face-to-face courses, and I think providing concrete examples of excellent student work could be particularly useful for those students who have a hard time understanding more abstract instructions and feedback from me. Now that I have taught the course twice, I also have examples of student writing that I can present as poor work without risking embarrassing the student who wrote it.

Finally, the next time I teach the course I'm going to revise the "warning" section of the syllabus in which I explain that online courses provide unique challenges to students. I already include a paragraph noting the need for greater self-discipline in online versus face-to-face courses. I plan to add a paragraph noting that students who have difficulty in online courses are those who do not have good reading comprehension, who do not like to read, and who do not write very well. Although this may seem obvious, it apparently isn't obvious to students. I suspect that many students are attracted to online courses because they expect them to be easy, and many are surprised when they realize the amount of reading and writing required. Both of my online courses had very high rates of student drops, which I do not experience in my face-to-face courses. I've asked students for suggestions for improving the course, and two of the three suggestions I got related to the difficulty of learning by reading alone—one student asked for PowerPoint slides to help explain material covered in readings. I suspect that many students have become accustomed to large lecture courses in which they don't complete the assigned readings and merely take notes from PowerPoint slides. I think it will be helpful for students to be told very explicitly that online courses are not like that, and that there are definitely types of students who are likely to do poorly in online courses.

Problem Two: Students do not read instructions or comments on their work. One of the most surprising things that happened the first time I taught *Crime and Delinquency* online is that about two-thirds of the way through the course, a student sent me an angry e-mail demanding an explanation of his grade on the second exam. It turns out that this student hadn't seen any of the comments I had made on any of his assignments during the course, including his first exam—he had only seen his grades. Because it had never crossed my mind that students would not expect comments on their work, it never crossed my mind that I had to point out to them that I was making comments on their work, or that I might need to explain how to use the course software to access my comments. Obviously I was wrong about this.

Solutions to Problem Two. Although I find it annoying, there is a pretty simple solution to this problem—to bombard students with repeated reminders and instructions throughout the course of the semester, and to make it really easy for them to re-read important instructions that are included in different documents on the course website. For example, the second time I taught the online course, the university had switched to a different online teaching software package that uses a small font size and single-spacing as its default modes for student assignment submissions. For this reason (and because students seem to be increasingly likely to write solid blocks of text with no paragraphs), I required that students submit assignments double-spaced. Most students had no problem with this, but even after repeated pleas from me to double-space, a few students continued to submit their assignment single-spaced, which meant that I was actually copying their submissions into a word processing document, reformatting them, and then pasting them back into the assignment feature of the software so I could use the grading functions of the assignment feature to give them feedback in a convenient way. Finally, I instituted a rule that assignments submitted single-spaced would not receive credit. This worked for a couple of weeks, but the single-spaced assignments started showing up again. For the rest of the semester, then, I included a paragraph at the beginning of every assignment reminding students that single-spaced assignments would not receive credit, and the problem appeared to be solved.

Similarly, rather than referring students back to particular sections of the syllabus that outlined things like "how to write an effective answer to an essay question," I've found that it's better to copy and paste those instructions into comments on students' assignments or exams, making it more difficult for them to ignore your recommendations for re-reading certain things.

Problem Three: Students don't participate effectively in online discussions. I have had mixed success with students' participation in online discussions. Although some students make really excellent contributions, many do the bare minimum, or post comments that are wildly off-topic, that are simply repeating what others have said, or that demonstrate misunderstanding of the material or issues being discussed. This is a problem that can escalate overnight, literally—one student who posts a comment that is completely irrelevant to the issue at hand can lead an entire class discussion astray while I'm sleeping and not checking in. This is more likely to happen, of course, when the issues being discussed are controversial or sensational. The worst example of this was when I asked students to read an article about the murder of albinos in Tanzania, which is apparently motivated by cultural beliefs that concoctions made from the body parts of albinos can bring good luck. Students were supposed to be addressing the social structural and cultural forces that might motivate such murders, but I was greeted in the morning by a series of angry rants about how the United States government has to go over there and do something to put a stop to it.

Solutions to Problem Three. It's obvious that instructions for students' discussion posts need to be very explicit, and there are many readily available examples of good rubrics for grading discussion posts. I used a rubric shared by a colleague but, as with any such teaching aid, I found it necessary to revise it to address problems I experienced in my courses. One addition I made after the first time I taught online was to explicitly encourage students to redirect any other students who are getting away from the question at hand, and to make it clear that this is something that would contribute positively to their grade for the discussion. Some students have done this, sometimes successfully and sometimes not. This is more likely to be unsuccessful when other students are not reading all of the previous comments in the discussion, and I've found that I have to repeatedly remind students that this is a requirement for participation in discussions.

I also learned that it's crucial to establish multiple deadlines for discussion posts, because many—if not most—students will wait until the last minute to post to the discussion, which of course makes real "discussion" very difficult. During the Spring 2010 semester, I had two discussion deadlines per week, which means that everyone is required to post early in the week, enabling subsequent discussion. More frequent deadlines would be even better, but I find this impossible to do in a five-week summer course that already requires students to post twice every day, Monday through Thursday.

Finally, I think it's important to emphasize to students that both quantity and quality matter in online discussions. I've been surprised at how often some students don't meet the minimum requirements for number of posts, including students who make excellent contributions to the discussion but then end up with a failing grade because they only posted once.

Setting more than two deadlines might also help keep students in the habit of checking in with the discussion on a regular basis.

ADDITIONAL RECOMMENDATIONS

I conclude with some recommendations to avoid other, more minor problems that are fairly simple to address.

Technical difficulties. I constantly hear about how tech-savvy our students are. Don't believe it. Even very basic information, like how to open .pdf documents, has tripped up some of my students. When beginning an online course, take the time to write detailed instructions about how to access course material. I have also made it explicit in my syllabus that computer problems are not an acceptable excuse for late or missed work (with the exception of problems on a system-wide scale, of course). I also begin the semester with a "practice" discussion posting that requires students to submit a low-stakes assignment to be sure they can use the software. This helps those students who have been enrolled from the beginning of the course, but students that add the course late miss this opportunity.

Lack of availability of films online. There are several educational films that I use in the classroom, which are available on DVD from the university library. However, the films I normally use are not available online. I have been frustrated in my efforts to find good-quality films online to replace them; sometimes they "appear" and "disappear" online, which is even more frustrating. However, many films are increasingly available in streaming video, and the university library has started to acquire subscriptions to some of them. If there are films you find indispensable for your courses, I recommend that you try to obtain them in streaming video from your institution before teaching online.

It's hard to prepare for online teaching without doing it. The semester-long series of workshops I participated in at URI during the Spring 2009 semester was absolutely invaluable in helping me prepare for teaching online. It was an excellent opportunity to learn from the experiences of others, and it gave me a chance to try out some of what I was learning with the courses I was teaching that semester. I held several online class "meetings" that semester, and this allowed me and my students to make some mistakes when the overall stakes were low. For example, I had one of my 300-level classes "meet" online for a class period, and I was upset to see that only a couple of students had actually posted to the online discussion like I had asked them to. But when I went to class to yell at them, it turns out that most of them had posted, they just posted in the "chat room" instead of where I had instructed them to post. This was my first lesson in the increased importance of detailed instructions for online courses.

Online courses are a lot of work. This may be more obvious to online teachers than it is to administrators who are looking at the bottom line, but in my opinion, the absolute maximum number of students one should take in an online course is twenty. I have a colleague at another university who is required to take thirty students in online courses, and she is getting pressure to take more. I don't think it's possible to teach a high-quality course online with written assignments, graded discussions, essay examinations, and lots of instructor feedback with more than twenty students, unless there are teaching assistants available to help with grading.

REFERENCES

Bernard, T. J., Snipes, J. B., & Gerould, A. L. (2010). *Vold's theoretical criminology* (6th ed.). New York: Oxford University Press.

Erickson, B. L., Peters, C. B., & Strommer, D. W. (2006). *Teaching first-year college students.* San Francisco, CA: Josey-Bass.

Felson, M., & Boba, R. (2010). *Crime and everyday life* (4th ed.). Los Angeles, CA: Sage.

Bureau of Justice Statistics. (2010). *Sourcebook of criminal justice statistics.* Retrieved from http://www.albany.edu/sourcebook/

Wright, R. T., & Decker, S. H. (1997). *Armed robbers in action: Stickups and street culture.* Boston, MA: Northeastern University Press.

CHAPTER 7

INTRODUCTION
TO SOIL SCIENCE

Transforming a Problem-Based Learning
Course to Online

José A. Amador

Problem-Based Learning (PBL) is an effective pedagogical approach that relies on groups of students solving open-ended, authentic problems, a process that leads to students learning the course content thru discovery. The PBL cycle—What do we know? → What do we need to know? → How are we going to learn it?—requires effective intra- and inter-group discussion, as well as instructor feedback, for students to learn the course content. In this chapter I describe the process of transforming a live, bricks-and-mortar PBL course—Introduction to Soil Science—into its asynchronous, online version, and discuss the opportunities and limitations presented by teaching the course in an online environment.

Introduction to Soil Science (NRS 212) is a 3-credit course taught in the Department of Natural Resources Science at the University of Rhode Island. The course has no pre-requisites. It is required for undergraduate students majoring in Environmental Science and Management, Environmental Economics and Management, Wildlife and Conservation Biology, Envi-

Taking Your Course Online: An Interdisciplinary Journey, pages 79–91
Copyright © 2012 by Information Age Publishing
All rights of reproduction in any form reserved.

ronmental Horticulture and Landscape Architecture. Although students are advised to take the course in their sophomore year, most students are juniors and seniors. A few undergraduate students from other disciplines also take the course because it fulfills the Natural Science requirement for General Education. Non-majors and graduate students generally make up fewer than 10% of the students. The class is always taught face-to-face one semester during the academic year, and has occasionally been taught during a 5-week summer session.

THE BRICKS-AND-MORTAR CLASS

I taught NRS 212 face-to-face using a traditional lecture format for about a decade. More recently I adopted a Problem-Based Learning (PBL) approach to teaching Introduction to Soil Science (Amador & Görres, 2004; Amador, Miles, & Peters, 2007). I was attracted to PBL as a teaching method partly because of its success in medical education (Neufeld & Barrows, 1974), a field similar to soil science in terms of its integrative, interdisciplinary approach to problem solving. A discipline like soil science requires that students draw from their knowledge of mathematics and basic and applied science—physics, chemistry, biology, ecology and geology—to understand the properties of soils and the processes that take place within them (Amador & Görres, 2004). The problems that professional soil scientists work on are generally complex, ill-defined, and require that the individual develops the ability to apply knowledge in the proper context. Finally, problems that involve soils are often addressed by teams of individuals with different professional training, such that successful solutions require not only technical knowledge, but the ability to communicate this knowledge effectively to experts and non-experts alike. The PBL approach has earned some praise from the academic community as an exciting, new way to teach introductory soil science (Baveye & Jacobson, 2009).

Enrollment in the face-to-face PBL version of Introduction to Soil Science varies from 40 to 50 students. They work in permanent groups of four or five to solve five real-life, open-ended problems over the course of the semester. Class time is spent primarily working on the problems. The problems are delivered in stages, and all the problems share the same structure. The first part of the problem includes (i) the title (usually something humorous, catchy or enigmatic); (ii) a schedule of activities (dates for discussion of different sections, exams, due dates for papers); (iii) a list of Learning Objectives, or what students are expected to learn as they work thru the problem, drawn from a list published for professional soil scientists by the Soil Science Society of America (Soil Science Society of America, 2010); (iv) a list of print and web resources; and (v) the first part of the problem narrative, along with guiding questions. The subsequent sections of the problem continue the narrative, with guiding questions at the end of each.

Once students are finished working on a problem, I ask them to (i) write a group paper ("synthesis paper") that describes their solution to the problem, (ii) take an in-class exam (with individual and group stages), and (iii) evaluate each other's performance as group members. Course grades are based on these assessments, with group papers and exams accounting for 40% and 60% of the course grade, respectively.

The course has a web site that serves as a repository for all class materials, provides a means for communicating class-related announcements to students, and gives students access to their grades. The course syllabus, problems, guidelines for preparing synthesis papers, and the rubric that I use to grade them, are also posted on the web site. The site is not interactive, since information generally flows from me to the students.

A TYPICAL CLASS SEQUENCE

On the first day of class I randomly assign students to groups and hand out the first part of the first problem. I then ask the students to go through a PBL cycle, which I describe for them (and they repeat throughout the semester). The cycle involves the following steps (Boud & Feletti, 1997):

1. Present students with a problem. Students assess the problem and identify what they know in relation to the problem.
2. Determine what aspects of the problem they do not understand. These "learning issues" serve to focus group discussion.
3. Rank learning issues in order of importance. The group decides which issues will be considered by the whole group or by individuals. In the case of individual follow-up, that student is then responsible for informing the rest of the group about his/her findings.
4. Explore previous learning issues and integrate new knowledge in the context of the problem. Students summarize their progress, make connections between previous and newly acquired knowledge, and develop new learning issues.

These steps are repeated until the group agrees that they have developed a satisfactory solution to the problem. The cycle can be abbreviated, as suggested by Pennell & Miles (2009) as: What do we know? What do we need to know? How are we going to find it out?

The PBL cycle is at the center of learning in this class. Students learn the course content as they progress thru the different stages of the cycle. The problem provides students with a reason to learn the course content (they need to gather and understand the information to solve the problem) and a context for learning (solving a real-world problem in soil science). In the process, they also develop their ability to gather, evaluate, and integrate information to solve problems, and to communicate this information to others in oral and written forms. The long-term goal is for students to internalize this approach to learning and apply it in their professional lives.

Groups initially have to come to a consensus as to what sorts of things they know and what they need to know. Once discussions within groups are finished, students present their lists of things they know and need to know, and explain their connection to the problem to the rest of the class. Students are encouraged to ask questions of the presenters. They then return to their groups to incorporate the information presented into their discussions, and develop plans for getting additional information.

During the next class period students share the information they have gathered with their groups and incorporate it into their solution to the first part of the problem. Groups then present their solution(s) to the rest of the class. Once the students (and I) are satisfied with the solutions, I hand out the next part of the problem, and the PBL cycle starts again.

ASSESSMENTS

At the end of each problem students write a group paper describing the problem and their solution(s) to it. One student is in charge of editing the paper, which can be revised based on my comments for a better grade. The roles of editor and reviser are rotated through the semester.

Students also take an in-class, multiple choice exam—based on the Learning Objectives—to assess their mastery of the subject. The exams have two parts. In Part One students have 60 minutes to answer the questions on their own. Immediately after turning in their individual answers, they meet for 25 minutes with their fellow group members to answer the same test.

Every student receives a peer evaluation from their group members, which assesses their willingness to participate in discussions, preparedness, and so on. The grade in the group paper is multiplied by the peer evaluation score to arrive at the grade for the individual student.

THE ONLINE VERSION

I have taught the online version of NRS 212 twice, during the 10-week summer session in 2009 and 2010. Enrollment has ranged from nine to 12 students—considerably fewer than for the classroom version. The class is conducted exclusively online and asynchronously.

I have retained as much of the structure and content of the face-to-face version as possible for the online version of the class. The problems I use are the same as those in the classroom version, although I have had to modify the narrative to fit the more compressed time frame of a summer course. For example, instead of four or five parts, all the problems in the online class have two parts. The Learning Objectives within each problem have remained the same, as have the guiding questions associated with each problem. I continued to ask students to write a group synthesis paper at the end of each problem and to submit peer evaluations of their performance as group members. Individual exams remain part of the course.

The transition from bricks-and-mortar to online was eased by the fact that essentially all class materials were already in a web-ready format, since I was used to posting them on the class web site for the classroom version: the syllabus, problems, grading rubrics, and other materials were already available as HTML or .pdf files. I was already familiar with the course management software and with most of the functions (e.g., e-mail, bulletin board, grade book, uploading and downloading files) that I use for the online course. So, the logistical aspects of transitioning from the classroom to the web were relatively straightforward. The real challenge was in creating and sustaining the conditions that lead to an authentic PBL experience in an online, asynchronous environment.

I have found the syllabus to be one of the most important documents in the online version of the course: it sets the tone and expectations for the course and describes the pedagogical approach, which is new for most students. In the online environment, where interaction is limited to asynchronous, written communication, it is essential that I get this right from the start. I email the class syllabus to all the registered students approximately two weeks before the official start of the course. The syllabus for the online class is considerably more detailed than the one for the face-to-face version: I want students to be clear about what they are getting into—in terms of the online aspects of the class as well as the pedagogical approach—and what is expected of them. Thus, in addition to having the usual information (e.g., what the course covers, textbook, instructor information, deadlines), the syllabus includes a flowchart of the PBL cycle as it takes place in the online environment (Figure 7.1). In addition, I provide them with the details of how group and individual postings and paper are graded and how peer performance is evaluated.

I randomly assign students to groups of four at the outset of the class. However, attrition at the beginning of the course requires moving students around to other groups. About a week into the class group composition stabilizes, with groups comprised of two to four students. I ask groups to identify members that will serve as reporter, whose job is to summarize and

1. Part 1 of the problem is posted online.

2. Thru group discussion (electronically or otherwise), your group develops a list of (1) things you know that will be helpful in solving the problem and how they are relevant, and (2) things you need to know to solve the problem and how they are relevant.

3. The group Reporter collates all the information and posts a list of 5 things you know, 5 things you need to know, and how each is relevant to the problem (also known as the "KNTK" lists on the class Bulletin Board.

4. Individual students post substantive feedback on the lists posted by other groups.

5. Thru group discussion, your group develops specific, detailed answers to the problem based on the information gathered by group members and feedback from other students.

6. The Reporter from each group posts answers on the class Bulletin Board.

7. Individual students post substantive feedback on the answers posted by other groups.

8. Part 2 of the problem is posted online.

Figure 7.1 Flowchart describing the PBL process for the online version of Introduction to Soil Science.

post information for the group, as well as the editor and reviser of the synthesis paper.

One distinct difference between the classroom and online versions of the class is in the way students are graded. In the classroom version, the discussions to generate and examine lists of what students know, what they need to know, and solutions to the problem are an integral part of the class—indeed, they take up the bulk of class time—but students receive no credit for that work. A mixture of peer pressure, fear of poor evaluations, prodding by the instructor, and the need to put together a coherent group paper appear to serve as incentive for students to participate in class discussions. The lack of face-to-face interaction and the asynchronous nature of the online course eliminates some of these incentives. Thus, to encourage students in the online course to take part in the intra- and inter-group discussions that are essential to the PBL cycle, I award students points for group postings of lists of things they knew and things they needed to know, of answers to questions, and for postings from individuals providing feedback on these. This shifts the "worth" of class discussions from none in the classroom version to 66% of the course grade in the online version and, in my opinion, has resulted in an improvement in the quality of these interactions, as I discuss later.

A TYPICAL CLASS SEQUENCE

Students can earn a total of 120 points on each problem, of which 80 are based on online postings. The problems in the online class have only two sections. Things get started when I post the first part of a problem. This sets in motion the online PBL cycle, which in my class involves (i) intra-group discussions to generate lists of those things students know and those they need to know to solve the problem (abbreviated as "KNTK lists"), followed by (ii) a round of feedback on these lists from individual students, (iii) additional intra-group discussions to generate answers to questions, and (iv) a round of feedback on these answers from individual students. All postings are worth ten points. Once answers and feedback are posted, I collate all of the postings, parse them to look for loose ends, misinterpretations, misrepresentations, erroneous information, dead-end lines of thinking, and so on, and post my own feedback, doing my best to guide—rather than force—students in a particular direction.

The discussions to generate KNTK lists and answers to questions are carried out strictly in the context of individual groups. The means by which the discussions take place is left up to the students. Although I provide them with private "chat rooms" for live discussion, and private discussion forums for asynchronous discussion on the course web site, I do not require students to use these. Students have other means of exchanging information that may be more convenient, or that they may be more comfortable with (e.g., email, instant messaging, texting, phone, even face-to-face conversations if they choose), and I do not want to limit their interaction by constraining the means of communication. That said, those instances when students do use the class web site to conduct their discussions provide me with an opportunity to examine their interactions, because these are recorded and available to the instructor (and the students). I have found it enlightening to "peek" into these conversations: they give me a window into students' preconceived notions, level of understanding, thought processes, and so on, which helps me understand where some of their ideas originate and help me to identify the sources of misconceptions, novel arguments, or conflicts.

Once students decide on the contents of their KNTK lists, the group reporter posts the lists on the course bulletin board for the whole class to see. At that point, students have 24 hours to provide feedback in the form of individual postings. To get full credit, students have to make substantive comments on the materials posted by a group other than their own. For example, they can suggest alternative interpretations of data, point out erroneous assumptions, suggest other sources of information, or explain why they disagreed with a particular statement. A posting is worth ten points, and I decide how many points to award based on the content of the posting.

After discussing among themselves the feedback they received from their peers, I ask groups to put together answers to all of the guiding questions for that part of the problem. The reporter posts these answers 24 hours after feedback from individual students is posted. This posting can earn the group ten points. Once the answers are posted, individual students post their feedback within 24 hours, with a posting earning an additional ten points.

After answers and feedback are posted, I collate and parse all of the postings and post my own comments and suggestions. For example, I point out errors of fact, try to dissuade students from going down blind alleys, suggest avenues of inquiry that may be more fruitful, and provide reassurance when it is warranted.

ASSESSMENT

Students write a group synthesis paper at the end of every problem. I grade the papers, make suggestions for improvement, and give them an opportunity to revise the paper for a better grade. This is no different from the classroom version. However, in the online version the entire process—submission, feedback from instructor, revision, resubmission—is paperless. In addition, the grade in the paper accounts for a smaller fraction of the course grade (17%) than in the classroom version (40%).

Whereas in the classroom version exams have an individual and a group phase, in the online version exams are exclusively an individual effort, and students are allowed 48 hours to turn in their answers. This is partly in response to the compressed schedule imposed during the summer term, which, between group and individual postings, does not leave much time for the additional online discussion necessary for the group phase of exams. Exams account for 17% of the course grade, a lower proportion than in the classroom course in which exams accounted for 60% of the final grade.

Peer evaluations are an integral part of the online course, although the evaluation criteria have been adapted to the online situation. The peer evaluations for the classroom version emphasize class attendance, preparation for discussion, willingness to listen and contribute, to meet outside of class—all of which take place in a face-to-face context. By contrast, peer evaluations for the online course emphasize participation in group discussions, meaningful contribution to group postings, and timeliness of contributions. The first time I taught the online course, I used peer evaluation scores to adjust the grade on the group synthesis paper. However, since papers account for a lower portion of the course grade in the online class, the stakes were lower for students, which appeared to lead some to think their behavior as group members mattered little. To address this problem, I now use peer evaluation scores to adjust all of the students' grades for a particular problem. This makes students acutely aware of the importance of being a good group member.

OPPORTUNITIES AND CHALLENGES

The dynamics of classroom discussions—the real-time give and take among students, my questions to guide the discussion, the interjections and challenges from other students, and so on—are, of course, absent in the online version. The pace of the online discussions is glacial by comparison: discussions that took place in a couple of class period in the classroom are spread out over a couple of days in the online class. However, what is lost in speed and spontaneity is gained in reasoned discourse and debate. Whereas in the classroom version students sometimes come up with half-baked, scattered ideas and arguments, students in the online class have more time to think, distill and integrate information—and it shows. As a result, KNTK lists are substantially more complete and focused, the information presented is more directly relevant to the problem, and student's arguments are better articulated. The answers posted are better developed than those presented by even the best groups in the classroom. In the face-to-face class there is little material incentive for students to provide feedback, such that the amount and quality of it tends to be uneven. By contrast, feedback from students in the online course is consistently more reasoned, useful, and plentiful, since they are getting points for providing it. The shift towards making discussion worth a significant fraction of the course grade—along with the additional time students have to research and reflect on the information—helps to raise the level of discourse in the online course.

The asynchronous nature of the course also allows me enough time to reflect on class discussions. In the classroom I have to react to statements on the spot, or provide guidance based on my recollections of who said what when during class discussions. In the online version it is all there, in black and white, for me to parse and evaluate, with enough time to think about the feedback I want to provide. This allows me to better ascertain what students do and don't get, to provide more focused feedback, to reference, challenge or support specific statements or arguments, to draw on examples from posted materials on what to do (or not). This sort of feedback also has the benefit of improving the quality of synthesis papers in terms of the content and the arguments made by students.

This is not to say that things always go smoothly in the online class. Many of the problems I observe in the classroom are also present online class, and in some cases these can be exacerbated by the online environment. Communication among group members is a good example. Timely and effective communication among students—to exchange ideas, provide and incorporate feedback, ask questions, and so on—is fundamental to the success of a PBL course, regardless of how it is taught. However, this is even more important in an online situation where communication is limited by the asynchronous nature of the course and the restrictions imposed by electronic means of communication. I had anticipated that this could present a problem online, so I purposely provided numerous warnings at the beginning of the class—and reminders throughout the course—of the fact that most communication is non-verbal and, in an environment where there are no visual or aural cues, students have to be especially careful with what they write. I also stress the fact that they cannot expect an instantaneous response to their electronic queries, whether from me or their fellow classmates: they have to plan ahead and be patient. Although most students heed this advice, it is ignored by some, and in a few instances I have found myself refereeing between group members about perceived slights or insults that stemmed from poor communication.

The dynamics of group work can also pose a greater challenge to students in the online course. Group work can be tough to negotiate, particularly for undergraduate students who are used working at their own pace and setting their own goals without having to consider the needs of others. Most undergraduate students have also grown up in an educational system where learning is structured by the instructor, who decides what students will learn and when. The student-centered, seemingly unstructured nature of PBL, combined with the emphasis on group work, can be trying for many students, particularly those that are less emotionally and intellectually mature. The absence of conventional structure in a face-to-face class tends to throw the less experienced students for a loop. These difficulties can be magnified in the online environment. For example, in some instances students "disappear"—do not answer messages, take part in group discussions or post feedback—only to resurface a few days later, explaining that they had gone on a long-planned vacation and simply forgot to inform fellow group members. This sort of irresponsible behavior is punished by other students—in the form of low peer evaluation scores—but can make subsequent group interactions more difficult.

IF YOU ARE THINKING OF DOING THIS...

- *The syllabus is key.* Make sure it is thorough and clear. Give it to a colleague or, better yet a student or someone who has had no experience taking a course online. Then ask them to describe the course expectations and mechanics to you. This will help you spot missing information, inaccuracies and misinterpretations.
- *Consider how you want the PBL cycle to play out in your course.* For example, you may want to separate things a bit more (e.g., have groups post "Things we Know" lists, followed by feedback from individual students, then have groups post "Things we Need to Know," followed by feedback, etc.) or extend these lists to include more items. Whether you want to (or can) do this may be constrained by time as well as the number of students taking the course, given that the feedback you provide students will require you to read and evaluate all of the posted materials.
- *Describe the online PBL cycle in excruciating detail.* Once you've decided how you want things to play out, give the students plenty of details— and time to digest them before the course starts. Flow charts probably work better than simple written descriptions. You may want to provide both in order to address different learning styles. Whatever you do, be explicit. Have an outsider read it and explain it to you, as I suggest for the course syllabus. They can help you spot the weaknesses in your description.
- *Adapt existing PBL problems to the online environment.* If you have been using PBL to teach your classroom course, you already have problems that you know work well. So, before you start to write a bunch of new problems, consider adapting those that you already have. In most cases it may just be a matter of abridging (or extending) the narrative, rephrasing the guiding questions, or altering the timeline.
- *Keep up with postings.* If you read the postings periodically, not only can you intervene quickly when you spot egregious errors of fact or logic (or when discussion turns discordant), but you can also start to formulate the feedback you will provide students. This beats getting to the end of a problem to discover that your students decided to pursue a line of inquiry that led them nowhere near where you were hoping they would get.

  I also find it enlightening to "peek" into the online conversations among group members: they give me a window into students' preconceived notions, level of understanding, thought processes, and so on. This helps me understand where some of their ideas originate and I believe enables me to provide better feedback on discussion postings. If you are going to do this, you need to tell students about it upfront, so they are aware that their conversations are not private.

- *Communication is key.* Effective communication—among students, between instructor and students—is imperative, both for learning the course content using PBL and for the smooth operation of an asynchronous, online course. As the instructor, you want to remind students early and often about the need for clear, respectful and timely communication, and how to avoid potential pitfalls. As the web site administrator, you will probably have access to communications within groups. Monitor these, as well as bulletin boards where feedback is posted, frequently and feel free to try to clear problems up right as they start to develop. It can save you and your students a lot of headaches later.

- *Be mindful of the shift in grading.* The shift in emphasis from grades based entirely on tests and papers to grades based primarily on online discussion postings may be new to you and your students. This shift may, as I pointed out earlier, improve the level of discussion associated with the various stages of the PBL cycle. Be aware, however, that students may put proportionally less effort into tests and papers. There are other instances where this shift may have unintended consequences. For example if, as was the case in my online course, peer evaluations are tied to the grade on group papers, lowering the contribution of group papers to the final course grade may also lower the incentive to be a good group member.

- *Enjoy the change.* The online PBL course is a different experience for the student and the instructor. The pace and the level of discussion are but two of the better aspects of the online PBL experience relative to the classroom.

REFERENCES

Amador, J. A., & Görres, J. H. (2004). A problem-based learning approach to teaching introductory soil science. *Journal of Natural Resources and Life Sciences Education, 33,* 21–27.

Amador, J. A., Miles, E. A., & Peters, C. B. (2007). *The practice of problem-based learning.* Bolton, MA: Anker Publishing Co.

Baveye, P. C., & Jacobson, A. R. (2009). Comment on "A soil science renaissance" by A.E. Hartemink and A. McBratney. *Geoderma, 151,* 126–127.

Boud, D., & Feletti, G. (1997). *The challenge of problem-based learning.* (2nd ed.). London: Kogan Page.

Neufeld, V., & Barrows, H. (1974). The McMaster philosophy: An approach to medical education. *Journal of Medical Education, 49,* 1040–1050.

Pennell, M., & Miles, E. A. (2009). "It actually made me think": Problem-based learning in the business communication classroom. *Business Communication Quarterly, 72,* 377–394.

Soil Science Society of America. (2010). Soil Science Performance Objectives—Fundamentals Exam Performance Objectives. Retrieved April 13, 2010 from https://www.soils.org/files/certifications/fundamentals-exam-objectives.pdf

CHAPTER 8

CREATING A FIRST ONLINE COURSE IN THE MATHEMATICS DEPARTMENT

James Baglama

Creating an online mathematics course for the first time can be a daunting task. In this chapter I share my experience of creating the first online mathematics course offered by the University of Rhode Island. I describe how I chose a face-to-face math course to translate into a successful online course, the pedagogical strategies used, lessons learned, and ideas for improvement. As in a face-to-face class the key to the success of the course is frequent communication, both between the student and instructor and among the students. I also discuss the techniques I used to make sure this important communication was carried over into the online course.

In the spring of 2009, the University of Rhode Island (URI) presented an opportunity to the faculty to transform a face-to-face course into an online course by offering a faculty fellows program for online teaching. At that time, the mathematics department did not offer any online math courses. Seizing the opportunity, I became the math department's first faculty fellow for online teaching. My initial task was to select a face-to-face class that I thought could be successfully transformed into an online course. Without access to an established online URI math course to use as a model, I wasn't entirely sure what courses would and would not work online. As such, my

Taking Your Course Online: An Interdisciplinary Journey, pages 93–100
Copyright © 2012 by Information Age Publishing
All rights of reproduction in any form reserved.

first step was to set up some criteria for selecting the course. After some re-flection, I determined that the course should be: (i) one that I had taught before, (ii) it should not be a course that is a prerequisite for another class nor contained in a sequence of classes, (iii) it should not require exten-sive math equations or graphing, and finally, (iv) the course should already have a lot of flexibility built into it.

My rationale for selecting a course I had already taught was that I did not want to risk the potential pitfalls of teaching a class for the first time while simultaneously transforming it into an online course. For example, teach-ing a class the first time requires finding a textbook that works well with the students, typing up new notes and digital presentation slides, testing out which examples are good examples, which homework problems are easy/hard, and which homework or concepts require extra clarification. If I did not pick a course I had already taught before, this would have added to the complexity of teaching the class online.

My second criterion—that the course not be a prerequisite for another class nor be contained in a sequence of classes (e.g., Calculus I, II, and III)—was based on the fact that there are certain benchmarks that must be met by the end of these courses in order for the students to be successful in the next course. This is not to say that these types of courses should not be offered online, but I felt that this type of course should not be chosen as a first online math course since I would be exploring which pedagogical methods work best online.

An online course requires students to submit their homework, quizzes, and questions online. Before I picked a course that required many math-ematical symbols (e.g., Calculus, Linear Algebra), I had to think about the medium that would be used to communicate between the students and me. Mathematicians have very little trouble reading and writing mathematical symbols across the different courses, but a student who is seeing these sym-bols for the first time will likely have difficulty reading and writing them, especially if they are presented online and are not formatted to match the textbook. Most students have access to some type of word processor, but the process required within the word processor to create symbols, such as an integral sign or fractions, can be tedious. Using a word processor as a mathematical sheet is inadequate for almost all math courses. Because my only contact with the students would be online, I would also have to provide corrections on these virtual homework sheets. For these reasons, I chose a class that requires few mathematical symbols and experimented with differ-ent types of online submissions.

Finally, I wanted a course that had a lot of flexibility already built into it. Generally, special topics or survey courses meet this requirement, since they typically do not have a standard textbook and cover many different topics.

This type of course allows the instructor to experiment with different topics while trying new online teaching methods.

The URI math department offers a course that satisfies all of the above criteria, MTH 108—Special Topics. This course satisfies the general education requirement for math at URI. The course content varies from section to section, semester to semester, and instructor to instructor. It is intended for students majoring in the liberal arts or other fields that do not have a specific mathematics requirement. The only prerequisite is a basic high school algebra background. Out of all of the math courses our department offers, MTH 108 was the obvious choice to transform from a face-to-face class to an online class. I have taught the course several times, and it is not a prerequisite for any other math course. There are no algebraic equations to solve and no integrals or derivatives to work out. Instead, this course focuses on real life applications: for example, voting strategies, identification numbers, Euler circuits, Internet searches, and mortgage payments. Quoting a student in my Spring 2010 online MTH 108 class, "this gets away from the black and white of math and adds a different aspect, which makes it more interesting, at least to me." Since a special topics course at URI can be given any name depending on the instructor, I titled my online course "Practical Mathematics."

Now that I had selected a math course to transform to online, I determined how I would set up the course. The main issue for consideration in transforming this course from face-to-face to the electronic format was the method of communication. I had to consider how to take a course in a discipline that requires extensive verbal communication between student and instructor, and transform it into one using written communication. In a face-to-face math class an instructor can oversee how a student is working out the problem via in-class work or by grading the student's homework. The instructor can also lay out all of the required steps in a lecture while simultaneously interacting with the audience and addressing their questions. This interaction with the audience is essential, and I wanted to include this important pedagogy into my online course. According to Engelbrecht and Harding (2005), communication in an online math course is the driving force behind its success. In a face-to-face class, a student communicates to you what they know by asking questions in class, handing in homework, or taking a quiz. You communicate back to them by answering questions in class and providing written feedback on the quiz or homework, indicating what is right or wrong. The question faced by the instructor is how do you simulate this essential communication online?

First, you need to have a reliable web-based system to facilitate communication. Simply creating a webpage and placing course material on it will not work for a math class. According to Selden and Selden (1997), mathematical knowledge is acquired by construction, not by transmission alone.

The web-based system must include many educational tools to engage the students. URI currently uses the system Sakai, which has a full range of tools required to run a successful online course (see http://sakaiproject. org/ for details on the tools). Swan et al. (2000) state that the interface should be transparent, easy to use and navigate. A fancy website with too much material or impressive videos to entertain the students is thought by some to be a waste of time (Stiles, 2000; Engelbrecht and Harding, 2005). My online website within Sakai is simple and the number of tools I use is kept to a minimum (Figure 8.1).

The primary tools that I use within Sakai are *Announcements, Assignments, Forums/Discussions, Gradebook, Messages, Modules, Schedule, Site Info, Site Stats, Syllabus, Quizzes,* and *Course Content.* Students in an online class need constant reminders of the assignments, similar to writing the assignments and due dates on the chalkboard every class period. The *Announcement* tool sends emails to students every time a new announcement appears. The *Schedule* tool—an electronic calendar—appears at the bottom right of the course page (Figure 8.1). When students log in to the website, they are shown what is due that week and a description of the assignments. Announcements and Schedule are set up prior to the start of the course and send automatic reminders via email to the instructor and students.

The *Modules, Syllabus,* and *Course Content* tools help give structure to the course. Bouncing from topic to topic or skipping around in the textbook may be OK for the instructor, but this can be confusing to the student if it is not laid out beforehand. *Modules* contain the plan for the entire class at

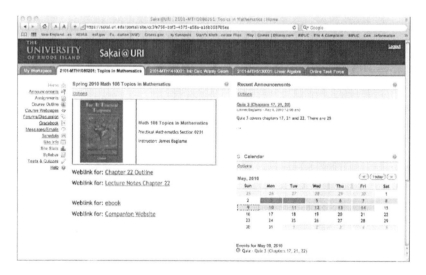

Figure 8.1 Snapshot of my Sakai website for the online MTH 108 course.

the start of the semester, along with links to the individual webpage for each chapter covered. For my course, I created a webpage for each chapter. In each webpage, I included all the important materials and assignments associated with that chapter, such as reading assignments, homework assignments, discussion topics, due dates, and links to digital presentations that I used in my face-to-face class (Figure 8.2). In addition, the chapter web pages are linked from many different sources within Sakai so that it very easy for students to find them.

So far, I have described the sections of my website where I make class materials accessible to students. What about the sections where communication between student and instructor take place? As stated before, communication is the key to a successful online course. As aptly noted by Engelbrecht and Harding (2005), "When designing an online offering, planning the communication to support learners can be just as important as designing the course material and presentation of that material" (pp. 259–260). I use the *Assignments, Forums/Discussions, Gradebook,* and *Messages* tools to communicate directly with students.

My first attempt at collecting homework was a disaster. I was using email, printing out the homework, correcting the homework, scanning the homework in, and then emailing the assignments back to the students. Emails got lost in the spam filter, students often sent assignments at different times, and I would have assignments scattered throughout my email "in" box, often without a subject line or a decipherable student email address.

Figure 8.2 Sample webpage of my own design for the MTH 108 online course.

Printing and scanning the assignments cost valuable resources and took many more hours compared to the same face-to-face routine for homework assignments. To address this problem I now use the *Assignment* tool. All assignments are submitted and graded within the *Assignment* tool. Grading is done on the computer with an Adobe .pdf reader/writer program, or directly within the *Assignment* tool's instructor comment box. This tool simulates the essential communication in the face-to-face class that I mentioned earlier, where you indicate to students what is right or wrong on the quiz or homework, and why.

I typically use email to discuss grades and to elaborate on a topic or question that a student does not understand. Email is also restricted to the *Messages* tool within Sakai to avoid lost messages and spam filters. I send out emails to the students at least twice a week. For example, I remind them that they must participate in discussion boards, of when homework is due, or give hints on difficult problems. Feedback is essential for the learning process. In a face-to-face class feedback is typically given verbally or by writing comments on returned homework, quizzes, and exams The comment section of the *Gradebook* tool and the instructor comment section in the *Assignment* tool are great ways to give feedback to the students when they submit assignments, essays, or participate in discussions.

Collaborative processes, when done right, can be a very effective teaching tool (Swan et al., 2000). I use the *Discussion* tool as a collaborative teaching tool, and I believe the discussion boards are the driving force behind the success of the online version of MTH 108. Hawisher and Pemberton (1997) state that online courses are successful with accountable participation for online discussion. When I started to develop the course I shied away from discussion boards because I did not know what topics to use or how to get students to participate. However, I had often noticed students helping each other in face-to-face classes and wanted to offer this form of support online. To set up the discussion boards I post the first topic/question and allow suitable time (one week) for students to post a response. My grading rubric (Table 8.1) is designed to ensure that the postings on the discussion boards are worth a significant portion of the student's grade. Simply posting "I agree" will get them a zero. Students are required to post a response to my question, post another question based on the topic, and, most importantly, to interact with the other students by responding to the postings of other students. Posting only once will result in zero points. With a class size of 20 students, I have had up to 65 postings on a particular topic. For example, one section of the textbook we used covered the Traveling Salesman Problem (TSP) and ways to solve it. I posted the following question on the discussion board:

TABLE 8.1   Sample Grading Rubric for Forums/Discussions

Criteria	3 points	2 points	1 or 0 points
Response to Questions	Student responds to the posted questions with thoughtful ideas, uses concepts in the text, and post in a timely manner.	Student responds to the posted question in a way that does not clearly use the concepts in the text.	Student responds to the posted question but misses the main idea.
Participation	Postings encourage and facilitate interaction among members of the online community. Student responds to other postings.	Postings rarely interact with or respond to other members of the online community. Not actively engaged in the discussion.	Postings respond to questions posed by the instructor only. Students rarely post to the discussion boards.

The Traveling Salesman Problem is one of the most intensively studied problems in mathematics. Why? What is the history behind the problem? What are the applications? How would you improve the movie "Strategies for Solving the TSP" on the companion website, i.e., what would you do differently?

Here are some of the students' postings on the TSP problem:

Sure, using the nearest-neighbor algorithm is the quickest and easiest way to solve TSP but I agree with you. Finding a minimum cost Hamiltonian circuit may take a bit longer to figure out an efficient route, but it may be the cheapest route.

If you use the sorted-edges algorithm you would organize the edges by their weight, or length, which still would not provide a logical explanation to develop a more cost-effective route.

Unfortunately the nearest-neighbor algorithm isn't the most cost effective route. It seems as if the sorted-edges algorithm is a better idea than the nearest-neighbor.

The nearest-neighbor algorithm is the one recommended by the movie on the companion website; perhaps if the video used other methods such as the brute force method or the sorted-edges algorithm, it could better show how Hamiltonian circuits can be found.

After reading this problem I decided to do some researching of my own. I didn't know any other ways the TSP was used besides those stated in the book. Naturally I turned to good old Google and found some other cool things much like the bees. Neat website. I found the optimal route to visit all 30 Major League Baseball parks. My husband and I are hoping to visit most when we retire. Now I have the route mapped out!

The postings show an understanding of the topic and, more importantly, an interest. My favorite posting was from the first semester teaching the online course, when a student posted to another student, "Thank you for your posting, I now understand the concept."

When I set out to create my course, I did not want the online version of MTH 108 to be static. I did not want to simply post my notes and assignments, ask some multiple choice questions, and assign a grade without ever interacting with the students. Instead, I wanted the online version to be a dynamic course where I interacted with the students frequently. In the future I will try—and advise others to try—other forms of communications. So far my communication has been strictly asynchronous (e.g., email, discussion boards), but I could try synchronous (real time) communication using chat rooms. This can be done as virtual office hours or shared whiteboards. Additionally, I plan to add pre-recorded video segments of key lecture content to enhance digital presentations.

Based on my experience, you can transform a face-to-face mathematics course into an online course if you can successfully engage the students on a regular basis. The online version of MTH 108—*Practical Mathematics* has been a success, with a low dropout rate and class grade average comparable to the face-to-face class. Initially, my colleagues and I had some reservations about whether or not a mathematics course could be designed as an online course. Now, because of the popularity of the course, the URI math department has expanded the online offerings to include more sections of this course.

REFERENCES

{ref}Engelbrecht, A., & Harding, A. (2005). Teaching undergraduate mathematics on the Internet. *Educational Studies in Mathematics, 58,* 253–276.

Hawisher, G., E. & Pemberton, M. A. (1997). Writing across the curriculum encounters asynchronous learning networks or WAC meets up with ALN. *Journal of Asynchronous Learning Networks, 1,* 61–69.

Selden, A., & Selden, J. (1997). Should mathematicians and mathematics educators be listening to cognitive psychologists? Mathematical Association of America Research Sampler 2. Retrieved from http://www.maa.org/t_and_l/sampler/rs_2.html.

Stiles, M. J. (2000). Effective learning and the virtual learning environment. *EUNIS 2000: Towards Virtual Universities: Proceedings of the European University Information System 2000 Conference held at Info system 2000, Poznan, Poland Pozanan: Instytut Informatyki Politechniki Poznanskiej,* 171–180.

Swan, K., Shea, P., Frederickson, E., Pickette, A., Pelz, W., & Maher, G. (2000). Building knowledge building communities: Consistency, contact, and communication in the virtual classroom. *Journal of Educational Computing Research, 23*(4), 359–383.

SECTION III

THE PROFESSIONS

CHAPTER 9

DESIGN PROFESSIONS AND ONLINE INSTRUCTION

An Introduction to Landscape Architecture

Farhad Atash

The large face-to-face introductory courses in design professions are generally taught in a lecture format, with quizzes and exams used for student learning assessments. This chapter reflects my experience with transforming a large introductory course in landscape architecture from a face-to-face format to an online platform. Specifically, I discuss the current content and format of the online course as well as short- and long-term strategies to improve the online learning experience for students. For courses in the design professions, the online environment provides a unique opportunity to cover issues related to the human, built and natural environments in a format that maximizes the application of visual materials, photos and video clips. For those introductory design courses with large enrollments, the online learning environment provides an opportunity to include a more diverse mix of student learning assessments compared to courses offered in a classroom setting.

The development of online college courses and degrees is rapidly changing the nature of higher education as experienced conventionally in classroom and other face-to-face settings. Design professions such as Architecture,

Taking Your Course Online: An Interdisciplinary Journey, pages 103–112
Copyright © 2012 by Information Age Publishing
All rights of reproduction in any form reserved.
103

Landscape Architecture and Urban Design typically require a significant amount of teacher/student interaction and formal/informal project review in a studio setting. Therefore, the online environment may pose challenges to teaching upper-level and advanced design studio. For these courses, a hybrid approach that mixes face-to-face teaching with an online environment is more appropriate for student learning. The hybrid approach offers new opportunities for students to learn as well as share their design projects with other students and the instructor in an online environment. Moreover, the students can take advantage of the online environment to develop their design portfolios over time. The final electronic portfolio produced in the senior year can be posted online for the purpose of networking with a wide range of potential employers.

For the lower-level and introductory courses in design professions, the online format presents a new and unique approach to teach students in these majors, as well as those students interested in acquiring a background knowledge in the design professions. Small enrollment, face-to-face introductory courses (20–25 students) in design are generally taught in a format that mixes lectures with hands-on assignments and projects. The lectures cover the theories, concepts, principles and the process of design, while the assignments provide the opportunity to apply lessons learned in lectures and readings to one or more projects done individually or as a team. For these courses, the online and classroom/online hybrid approaches are good options to consider.

The large enrollment, face-to-face introductory courses (with 50 or more students) are generally taught in a lecture format. Quizzes and exams are generally used for the student learning assessments. Given the size of the class, hands-on assignments and projects are often not practical because of the amount of time required to interact with each student, especially with those that do not have a design background. For this type of face-to-face introductory design courses that are primarily lecture-based, teaching exclusively online provides a new and unique environment for learning. This chapter reflects my experience with transforming a large introductory course in landscape architecture (LAR 201) from a face-to-face format to an online platform.

The Bachelor of Landscape Architecture (BLA) degree at the University of Rhode Island (URI) is designed to train undergraduate students for professional careers in the public and private sectors. The profession involves the design, planning, preservation, and restoration of the landscape, applying both art and science to achieve the best use of our land resources. Landscape architects engage in the design and planning of parks and recreation areas, residential developments, commercial centers, public spaces, waterfronts, corporate and institutional campuses, transportation facilities and new communities.

Accredited by the American Society of Landscape Architects (ASLA), the newly revised Bachelor of Landscape Architecture at the University of Rhode Island requires a minimum of 126 credits. LAR 201—*Survey of Landscape Architecture*, is a three-credit required course for Landscape Architecture majors. Undergraduate students take LAR 201 in the first semester of their studies. The principal purpose of the course is to provide an introduction to landscape design theory and composition as an applied art form, and to study the relationship between the elements of the built and natural environments. The course is divided into five parts:

1. Introduction to the Landscape Architecture Profession
2. Landscape Architecture Profession and Future Challenges (Population growth and shifts, Global climate change, Energy crisis, Water crisis and Infrastructure crisis)
3. Elements of Landscape Architectural Design Plan (Landform, Plant Materials, Buildings, Pavement, Site Structures, Water and Circulation)
4. Elements and Principles of Design
5. The Design Process

LAR 201 is also listed as an elective for the fulfillment of the "Fine Arts and Literature" component of the General Education requirements at the university. In the past, the face-to-face version of LAR 201 course was offered every fall semester, with an enrollment capacity of 80 to 90 students. The course was enrolled to capacity every semester. Of the total enrollment in any given semester, 18 to 20 students were from the Landscape Architecture Department, with the remaining students from departments in different colleges, including the College of the Environment and Life Sciences (home of the Department of Landscape Architecture), Arts and Sciences, Engineering, Human Sciences and Services and Business Administration.

LAR 201 IN THE CLASSROOM

The face-to-face version of LAR 201 follows a lecture format to accomplish its major goal of providing an introduction to theory, elements and concepts of the landscape architecture profession. The course meets twice a week and each class session is 75 minutes long. Attendance is mandatory. The course requirements include three exams that have multiple choice, true/false and matching questions. Each exam covers about one-third of the course content. The first exam accounts for 30% of the course grade, while the second and third exams each account for 35% of the course grade. Given the large enrollment and diversity of students interests and backgrounds, no hands-on assignments and/or projects are included in the course.

Each lecture in the face-to-face version of the course includes a combination of texts drawn primarily from the required textbook, as well as a large number of visuals from the textbook and other sources. These include landscape architectural drawings (e.g., master plans, site plans, three-dimensional sketches, construction drawings, etc.) as well as photos of different projects in urban, suburban and rural settings. The combination of text, visuals and photos used in the lectures help to explain theory and the practice of the landscape architecture profession in the United States. The lectures, particularly the visuals and photos, are generally very well received by the students. The texts of all lectures are made available to student on the library electronic reserves. This helps students to focus their attention in the classroom on the lectures without worrying about taking notes. The availability of the lectures on the electronic reserves has also helped students to prepare for exams. Past Student Evaluation Teaching of the face-to-face version of LAR 201 indicates that the majority of the students are pleased with the quality of their learning experience.

The face-to-face version of the course has its share of limitations. Given the large enrollment in the course, the course requirements have been limited to three exams with multiple choice questions. The opportunity for detailed feedback and comments on the real examples of landscape architectural projects shown to students in class is limited by time constraints. Although I make a deliberate attempt to encourage student participation in class discussions, many students do not participate. Given the size of the class and the mix of students' backgrounds and skills in design and landscape architecture, many students may not feel comfortable asking and/or answering questions or expressing their opinions about a project. Some students have expressed an interest in having digital or hard copies of some of the visuals and photos used in the course. The large class enrollment has precluded me from fulfilling this request. Alternatively some students have had their own digital visuals and photos that they were willing to share for the use in class lectures. In the past, the visuals were frequently not submitted on time to fit into a lecture. The good news is that teaching the LAR 201 course online has the potential to overcome these and other limitations of the face-to-face version, as well as offer new learning opportunities for students.

THE ONLINE VERSION OF LAR 201

Similar to developing a new face-to-face course, developing an online course requires a significant amount of time. The process begins with defining course goals and outcomes. The course goals and outcomes shape the format of the online course, the components of the course and its student learning assessments. Every component of the course has to be designed in a manner that is easy for the students to understand and follow. For example, the course syllabus should clearly define the weekly schedule for the students and the due dates for the learning assessments such as assignments, quizzes and tests. The directions for assignments, quizzes and tests must also be presented in a logical and simple way.

It is suggested (Zhu, Payette, & DeZure, 2003) that when developing an online course, college instructors consider a number of major issues, including:

- Course content;
- Delivery of instruction;
- Communication and interaction; and
- Assessment of student learning.

"Course content" deals with the course coverage, appropriately defined instructional goals and objectives, effectiveness of learning activities and appropriateness of assessment methods. For courses in the design professions such as landscape architecture, the students learn best when the course content is presented visually (e.g., drawings, diagrams, maps, pictures, photos, video) and complemented with limited text that highlights key topics.

"Delivery of instruction" deals with the appropriateness of technology used to deliver course materials (e.g., digital presentations, video and audio clips, video conference, etc.), usefulness of course website and its design (e.g., structure, interface, navigation, instructions to online activities).

"Communication and interaction" covers issues dealing with adequate communication with students, availability to respond to student questions, frequency of feedback during the course, and means of feedback in the learning process. In short, an online course should provide plenty of opportunities for interaction and communication student to student, student to instructor and student to course content.

Lastly, "Assessment of student learning" emphasizes topics such as clear communication of the nature, duration, and due date of all planned assessment methods, employment of a wide range of assessment methods (e.g., tests, quizzes and exams, individual/group papers and projects), and alignment of assessment with course goals.

THE CURRENT CONTENT OF THE LAR 201 ONLINE COURSE

I offered the online version of LAR 201 for the first time in Summer of 2009. The enrollment capacity in the course was set at 20 students for each semester. In what follows, I describe the current content of the online course as well as the experiences and lessons learned from its delivery in three semesters: Summer and Fall semesters in 2009 and Spring semester in 2010.

I had two main goals for the online version of LAR 201. My short-term goal was to design the online course to be simple and user-friendly for the students. This was to make sure that all key educational components of the face-to-face version of the course could be delivered entirely online with minimum difficulties for the students to learn. In brief, my initial experience in offering the LAR 201 online course was successful and I did not experience any major problems.

My long-term goal is to refine and improve the online delivery of the course using a greater variety of content, types of visual materials and learning assessments. This will provide an opportunity to explore the application of new learning components in the online course that normally cannot be done (or done easily) in the face-to-face version of the course.

The online version of LAR 201 course has the same content and uses the same textbook used in the face-to-face version. The course requires eight quizzes and two exams. Quizzes account for 32% of the course grade. The mid-term and final exams are multiple choice and are worth 30% and 38% of the final course grade, respectively.

Each quiz has four essay questions and the students submit their answers online. The students have a week to take each quiz, but they have access to it only once, with no time limit. I post each quiz on the course website on a Saturday and have it due the following Saturday. This arrangement gives me the opportunity to grade the quizzes over the weekend and make the grades and feedback available to students by Monday morning. Late submissions are not accepted. In the face-to-face version of the course I have not used "quizzes" due to the large number of students in the class. The online format—and the lower number of students—provides a unique opportunity to use quizzes with essay questions as part of the learning assessment methods I use in the course.

The mid-term exam has 50 multiple choice questions with a two-hour time limit to take it online. The final exam has 70 questions with a three-hour time limit to complete it online. All questions are presented in one web page and the students can go forward and backward among the questions. Each exam is available on the course website for 24 hours on a selected day of the semester. This arrangement has worked well with all students given their different schedules. Each exam can be accessed only once and no late submissions are accepted.

The course is divided into 11 week-long units. For each unit, I developed an online lecture using text and visuals to complement the readings from the textbook. In addition, I posted selected photos of related landscape architectural projects on the course website. A short quiz is required for eight of the eleven units of the course. In summary, for each unit of the course, the students are asked to read a chapter of the required textbook, read a lecture, view a photo presentation of related design projects, and take an online quiz with four questions related to the topics covered in the respective course unit.

The main page of the course website is designed to be visually pleasing and easy to read and navigate. It includes the main tools of Sakai platform (see next paragraph), a weekly announcement that includes a list of activities for each unit of the course, a monthly calendar of main events as well as a notification box for email messages and forums. I also post two or three photos related to the course, which I change weekly. I believe the photos help to make the course website more visually appealing and encourage students to login to the course website more frequently. The course website includes the following tools on the Sakai platform: "Syllabus," "Schedule" (Calendar), "Announcements," "Modules," "Presentation," "Test and Quizzes," "Forums," and "Messages."

OBSERVATIONS AND LESSONS LEARNED FROM TEACHING LAR 201 ONLINE

Including the Spring 2010 Semester, I have taught LAR 201 online for three semesters. I have four general observations based on this limited experience. First, the online teaching experience has gone well without any major problems for me and the 57 students enrolled in the course in three semesters. Second, I did not receive any direct complaints from students regarding the nature of the online course. Third, no student failed the course; however, a small number of students in each semester received low grades because they did not take the quizzes and exams by the due date. Lastly, to the best of my knowledge, no student from outside the University of Rhode Island was enrolled in the online course.

Generally speaking, the communication between me and the students went well. Most students logged into the course website frequently to do their work and participate in class discussions on time. However, every semester two to three students did not do some of their work (e.g., weekly quizzes) on time because they failed to log in to the course website regularly. This confirms the belief that undergraduate students need to have sufficient self-discipline in order to do well in an online course. Without face-to-face contact between faculty and students, a small number of students fail to engage in the online course and keep up with the learning assessments.

The students did not report problems with downloading the lecture notes or viewing digital photos of selected projects. Overall, I received a number of positive comments about the use of digital photos in the course website.

In regard to the course learning assessments, the use of weekly quizzes helped to ensure the students followed up with the readings and logged in to the course website regularly. Taking the weekly quizzes also gave students a better idea of what type of questions to expect in the mid-term and final exams, as well as learning how to work with the "Tests and Quizzes" tool prior to taking exams.

According to Johnson-Curiskis (2006), "Research indicates that online, open book tests can be just as discriminating and can result in as much learning as traditional exams; therefore online unmonitored exams are appropriate for the college classroom" (p. 46). From my experience, I see a number of advantages to online exams. First, when using online exams for courses in design professions, the instructor can easily incorporate questions based on different types of visuals, including drawings and photos. Second, with online exams designed with automated scoring, students can receive immediate feedback. Third, the instructor can easily allow a student to retake a quiz or an online exam, or allow a student to make up a missed quiz or an exam.

Although no grade was given for participation in the online discussions in LAR 201 in the first two semesters, the majority of students were involved in online discussions. The highest level of participation was in summer of 2009. In the Spring of 2010 the participation was low due technical problems and changes with the use of the "Forum" in the Sakai platform. The level of voluntary student participation in the online course discussions has been greater than the face-to-face version of the course. This suggests that a typical undergraduate student feels more at ease commenting and asking questions in an online environment compared to a classroom setting. Moreover, because the student has the time to think before writing a comment and/or a question online, the quality of questions, answers and comments are in general better than those typically offered in the classroom. In short, the online environment has the advantage of giving the students the opportunity to be more engaged in the learning process by reading and writing commentaries.

There are other advantages to teaching online. For example, in the Spring 2010 semester, URI had to cancel all classes for four days due to snow and severe flooding, the worst experienced in the state in over 100 years. While the extreme weather had major impact on face-to-face courses and in classroom instructions, it did not interrupt the online courses, and the "distance learning" format proved to be a very desirable approach for both faculty and students.

SUGGESTIONS AND RECOMMENDATIONS
FOR THE FUTURE

Summer of 2010 will be the second year of teaching LAR 201 online. Looking into the future, I am considering a few changes for the second and third years of instruction (short-term) as well as major changes beginning in the fourth year of teaching (long-term) the course online.

Short-term, I am considering formalizing the participation in the online class discussions by assigning it a share of the course grade. I plan to post questions on each topic with a specified time limit for each student to respond. I will monitor the quantity and quality of responses received from each student during the semester to make sure that students are engaged in the course and allocate adequate time consistently during the semester to study the course materials. The time needed to engage in an online course exceeds the amount of time that a student spends in a face-to-face course because student participation involves writing and reading posts.

I am also considering having students upload photos of related landscape architectural design projects for bonus points. Appropriate photos will be posted on the course website, with credit given to the student. This change should make the course more interactive and fun for students.

Lastly, I am considering adding a number of digital video clips (e.g., YouTube) that highlight design elements, principles and process, as well as different case studies of landscape architectural design projects from across the country. This will complement the existing collection of photos and images that are used in the online course.

Long-term, I am looking for an appropriate e-textbook for the course. This will make it easier for all students (in Rhode Island and elsewhere) to buy and read the textbook online. Currently, the students enrolled in the online class can purchase the textbook from university bookstore (in person, by phone or online) or from vendors on the Internet.

In addition, I am considering adding a new requirement to the online course. This will entail posting a description, as well as photos, of a major landscape architectural design project on the course website. The students will be asked to evaluate the project and list its major advantages (assets) and disadvantages (drawbacks). This assignment could be done individually or in groups of three to four students. If the assignment is planned as a group effort, a greater interaction will be generated among students in the course.

Alternatively, I may incorporate a project that requires that each student to select and visit a "study area" of his/her choice (e.g., a park, a plaza, a residential subdivision), and survey it visually, including taking digital photos. The outcome of the site visit and project analysis will be uploaded on the course website for other students to see and comment on. With the addition of an authentic design project, the assessment of student online learning will be diversified beyond the quizzes and multiple-choice exams and include the evaluation of a landscape architectural project and participation in online class discussions.

CONCLUSIONS

Based on my online teaching experience, I agree with the conclusion drawn from the literature that "teaching and learning online are not better or worse than on campus, face-to-face teaching and learning—they are just different" (Johnson-Curiskis, 2006, p. 43). The online environment presents a unique opportunity for student learning across different disciplines. For courses in the design professions, the online environment provides a unique opportunity to cover issues related to the human, built and natural environments in a format that maximizes the use of visual materials, photos and video clips. With students having full access to these materials and resources during the course of the semester, the learning experience will be more meaningful and rewarding. For those introductory courses with large enrollments, the online learning environment provides an opportunity to include a more diversified mix of student learning assessments compared to a course offered in a classroom setting. For introductory design courses with small enrollments, the online environment can be an equally effective and powerful approach.

REFERENCES

Johnson-Curiskis, N. (2006). Online course planning. *MERLOT Journal of Online Learning and Teaching, 2*(1), 42–48.

Zhu, E., Payette, P., & DeZure, D. (2003). An introduction to teaching online. *CRLT Occasional Papers, 18,* 1–6. University of Michigan, Center for Research on Learning and Teaching.

CHAPTER 10

PROFESSIONAL PRACTICE IN HEALTH AND ILLNESS

An Online Transformation

Kara Misto

As a health profession, nursing has at its core profound human-to-human interaction, often caring for another human being during the course of an illness. This chapter describes the experience of transforming an introductory nursing course, Professional Practice in Health and Illness, *from a traditional face-to-face didactic to a complete online delivery. Following a description of the overall content of the course, the chapter then focuses on the transformation of each content area of the course online, including some of the creative strategies and adventures involved in the process. Finally, I discuss some of the advantages and challenges identified in online teaching and learning of concepts related to professional practice disciplines.*

While many academic disciplines have for some time embraced online learning as a significant portion of a student's curriculum, professional schools—especially nursing—have been somewhat slower to respond (Field, 2002; Kenny, 2002; Lashley, 2005). As a health profession, nursing has at its core profound human-to-human interaction, often caring for another human being during the course of an illness. This chapter describes

Taking Your Course Online: An Interdisciplinary Journey, pages 113–130
Copyright © 2012 by Information Age Publishing
All rights of reproduction in any form reserved.

the experience of transforming an introductory nursing course, *Professional Practice in Health and Illness*, from a traditional face-to-face didactic to a complete online delivery. Following a description of the overall content of the course, the chapter then focuses on the transformation of each content area of the course to online environment, including some of the creative strategies and adventures involved in the process. Finally, there is a discussion of the advantages and challenges identified in online teaching and learning of concepts related to professional practice disciplines.

As faculty begin to consider the prospect of transforming an introductory nursing course into one for online delivery, there are various teaching and learning considerations that must be explored. Careful planning is required for this type of transition. Planning for the online version of *Professional Practice in Health and Illness* course for online delivery was aided by my participation in an online faculty fellows program offered by the University of Rhode Island.

THE TRANSFORMATION

Nursing 103—*Professional Practice in Health and Illness* is a freshman nursing course offered through the University of Rhode Island's College of Nursing. The course is designed to meet the needs of beginning nursing students. Students generally participate in weekly lecture sessions that will assist them in developing an understanding about themselves as beginning health care providers, as well as the client's perspective of health care. Foundational concepts regarding health and illness are introduced as they pertain to professional health practice, with a significant focus on the nursing profession and the role of the registered nurse. Students explore the following major topic areas: group dynamics, stress, professional caring, culture, critical thinking and decision making, communication, values, ethics, and legal implications involved in health care, health, wellness and illness, the teaching and learning processes, and health care delivery systems within the context of the professional health care provider role. In the face-to-face version of this course, students are asked to participate in various classroom activities, including—but not limited to—games, role-playing, and case study presentations, in an effort to promote critical analysis of fundamental concepts for nursing. The objective for students participating in these types of activities, which promote hands-on learning, is that they will be able to practice and demonstrate some of the behaviors and responsibilities central to professional helping disciplines such as nursing.

Each of the major topic areas is a building-block essential to developing the professional skills needed for clinical nursing practice. During the online translation, modifications had to be made to some of the experiential learning activities. In addition, specific teaching methods needed to be employed that are fairly standard to online courses. The first was the use of online group discussions, which are common to most any web-based courses. Sometimes the discussion questions were based only on class content or readings, but very often they also included other types of media that could then be referenced in the weekly discussions. The questions were carefully planned to provoke critical thinking and reflect real-world application of topical concepts. Students were first asked to post answers to a series of questions and within a few days, they were asked to post a response to at least two other student postings. I developed a rubric to set expectations for online discussions (Figure 10.1).

Students were also assigned weekly readings specific to the course's scheduled discussion concepts. These readings were essential for learners to be able to comprehend the course content and were supported with a corresponding homework assignment. Expectations regarding weekly homework assignments were also outlined utilizing a rubric that was available for all students online (Figure 10.2). Supplementary online quizzes were included as another means of assessing comprehension of the weekly readings and content presentations. Additionally, there were larger assignments spread out throughout the 10-week session, including case studies, a process recording, and a cultural assessment.

CONTENT AREA: GROUP DYNAMICS

One of the first content areas explored in *Professional Practice in Health and Illness* is group dynamics and teamwork. This initial class asks for the students to gain knowledge regarding group processes first within the context of their world, and then to translate this knowledge to professional helping. Familiarity with group dynamics and teamwork is a basic skill that is essential in professional disciplines such as nursing. Nursing students must become proficient at working in groups and successfully demonstrate this as they begin their clinical practica where they will be required to do so effectively. Learning about group work in this course includes a well-developed classroom activity using a game called "Squares" in which students collaborate nonverbally in small groups to form squares from small pieces of paper. This exercise is beneficial because it draws parallels to the team precision and teamwork with which health care providers, such as nurses, must use when caring for a critically ill client. In order to transform this course into an online format, many of the assignments, like the squares game, required reconfiguration to support an on-line method of instruction.

It was a struggle to determine how to take such a powerful learning activity and somehow re-engineer it for online learning. Some activities just

NUR 103—Online Discussion Rubric

This rubric is designed to show the requirements for acceptable discussion responses. You may utilize it to develop an understanding of what I will be looking for from you in our weekly discussion postings. Each weekly discussion will be worth 2.5 points, equaling a total of 25 points.

Learning Outcome	Exemplary (2.0–2.5 points)	Accomplished (1.0–1.5 points)	Needs Work (0–0.5 points)
Relevance	Response of information which is accurate and related to discussion topic. Cites evidence/references which are relevant.	Response indicates understanding of the concept, but provides no evidence to support ideas. Doesn't invite further discussion.	Response was not applicable to the discussion, remarks were short; Did not provide evidence to support ideas.
Clarity/ articulation	Posting is easy to read with correct grammar; rare misspellings.	Several errors in grammar and spelling.	Utilizes poor grammar and spelling; post appears hastily done.
Position/Stance	Response expresses opinions and ideas clearly and concisely with obvious connection to the topic.	Response contains unclear convictions or is not related to the topic.	Response does not express ideas or opinions clearly; no connection to the topic.
Participation	Student responds to more than two other students in a way that makes connections through analysis and builds on others' ideas through meaningful discussion.	Student responds to other learners in a way that makes some connections, however they are shallow; does not enrich discussion.	Student does not respond to other learners, or responses are lacking in connections and meaningfulness.
Promptness	Responses were prompt; demonstrates good self-initiative.	Initial and follow-up responses were tardy and after due dates.	Did not respond to postings.

Figure 10.1 Online class discussion rubric for NRU 103.

NUR 103—Homework Assignment Rubric

This rubric is designed to show the requirements for homework assignments. You may utilize it as a guide to what would be expected in a homework assignment.

Learning Outcome	Exemplary (A)	Accomplished (B)	Needs Work (C)
Learning Demonstration/ Meaning of content	Answers clearly show that the student has completed learning activities in a manner which illustrates knowledge and understanding of the content.	Most answers are correct, may have a few areas which appear erroneous and may indicate a need for further reflection on content.	Answers reflect no comprehension of the assignment's covered content. Learning activities were obviously not completed.
Clarity/ articulation	Answers to questions are easy to read and understand; uses correct grammar and has only rare misspellings.	Several errors in grammar and spelling; is difficult to comprehend.	Utilizes poor grammar and spelling; disordered and not synthesized well at all.
Interpretations	Answers clearly express views and ideas with conciseness and obvious connections to the questions.	Explanations are somewhat unclear or convictions are not related to the topic.	Replies do not express ideas or opinions clearly; no connection to the topic.
Promptness	Assignment was handed in on due date; Demonstrates autonomy and accountability.	Assignment was slightly tardy, but student made effort to be accountable by contacting instructor.	Assignment was significantly late or not handed in, no demonstration of student accountability.

Figure 10.2 Homework rubric for the online version of NUR 103.

cannot be altered for web-based learning without losing the original context. Thus this content required a different method of delivery other than the "Squares" game that could still illustrate what working in groups is all about. To accomplish this, students were asked to watch the film *Apollo 13*, which was available at most public libraries, in addition to video rental stores and online movie rentals. This movie examines teamwork in the most critical of situations, and parallels to nursing teamwork can certainly be drawn. The students answered in-depth, specific questions tailored to evaluate participation in a formal group. The goal was to have students begin to identify and explain positive group behaviors.

To further assist in highlighting the necessity of strong teamwork, students were also directed to view an online movie/slide-show produced by two U.S. Navy Blue Angels' pilots, Scott Beare and Michael McMillan. The discussion posting regarding group dynamics asked students to first discuss a time they were a member of a formal group and to then critique the dynamics of this experience, based on what they had now learned about group structures and processes. Students were also asked to describe how the crew of the Apollo 13 demonstrated some of the effective features of a group and then more importantly, to begin reflecting on why this type of team activity and cohesion is essential in health care teams. As one student described:

> During... Apollo 13... it was important that the team was able to communicate well with each other, and that trust be built among them... Healthcare teams are an integrated network of qualified licensed personnel. It is crucial that trust is established, the environment is comfortable to work in, that each individual shares a common goal with their co-workers, and that they strive to accomplish that goal as a team...

CONTENT AREA: ANXIETY, STRESS AND FEAR

In this portion of the course students begin delving into the readings on stress, anxiety and fear. The readings describe stress as it relates to illness or situational factors and how it emerges physiologically and/or mentally and emotionally. Students are also taught some of the ways that nurses can intervene through prevention or coping mechanisms taught to clients under stress. Students then complete a homework assignment based on the readings and the instructor's presentation handout provided on the course website. It is important that students are able to recognize signs of anxiety, stress and fear of these issues in others, so that they can plan their care accordingly. Students are also asked to explore these concepts as they relate to their own stress, anxiety or fear, and how this may impact their own professional practice. The objective for this part of the course is for students to begin to identify the differences between anxiety, stress and fear, how each of these may cause one to feel threatened and, most importantly, how this may impact someone's health.

In the face-to-face course students read about stress, threat and anxiety, followed by a lecture on the same topics. The students then complete a series of stress scales. The online version of this course follows a similar format, however, it adds a second component to the homework, asking students to answer a series of questions regarding the identification and application of several theories related to stress. This additional homework component allows students to expand their knowledge through enhanced content analysis. In addition, the online version asks students to respond to one of two discussion postings regarding stress. Here is one example of a student posting:

> About a month ago my children, my husband and I were taking a drive in Newport . . . I was driving . . . My husband was drinking bottled water and all of a sudden appeared to be choking. He stopped breathing and turned dark blue . . . I was faced with a life and death situation. Immediately I could feel my heart racing, an adrenaline rush, and light headedness, as well as my breathing becoming heavier. I became anxious and felt a lot of stress . . . I feared that he would die . . . I called 911 . . . in the future I would try to remain calmer when conveying information that is critical . . . I understand now how important it is to be able to maintain composure when faced with a situation of life and death.

This type of reflection was representative of what most students posted and brought a dynamic focus to the dialogue of this course that is not usual in a typical classroom, either due to time constraints or student reluctance to talk in class. In a face-to-face class such personal reflections are scarce, as there rarely is enough time to have each student share such a comprehensive and compelling story. In addition, some students simply are not comfortable with public speaking and choose not to share.

CONTENT AREA: CARING AND HELPING/PROFESSIONAL ROLE RELATIONSHIPS

This section merges two different content areas; therefore the amount of material is vast. This is, however, a well-liked content area by most students because it is where the discussion of professional nursing roles begins. Students begin to discover the key components of a professional helping relationship and how this differs from a social relationship. They begin to identify what the various roles of a professional nurse might be—such as caregiver, educator, advocate, and/or manager—and the factors that influence the ways in which nurses practice. The face-to-face version of this content includes a presentation on helping relationships. Class discussions focus on the differences between caring in a social relationship versus a professional relationship, as well as how to establish a trusting, non-judgmental caring relationship. Additional discussions include the professional positions of nurses, what distinguishes nursing as a profession, and the multiple specialties in nursing, such as: education, certifications, as well as advanced practicing nursing roles. This class usually involves a very active discussion about what nursing is, why students may be interested in becoming a nurse and what it means to be a "professional" versus "having an occupation."

In the online course, students were asked to read the instructor presentation and read the relevant book chapters. In an effort to retain the valuable discussion that takes place in the face-to-face version regarding professionalism, students were also asked in their discussion postings to respond to an article regarding nursing professionalism. This article, by La-Sala and Nelson (2005), discusses that as nurses interact with clients, families, community members, corporate personnel, and policymakers, their appearance, behavior, dress, and communication skills are significant in projecting their professional image.

Students were also asked to view a video clip (which was available via the course website through a link) that discusses nursing roles, entitled "I'm Just A Nurse" (G. Raymond Chang School of Continuing Education, 2008). This clip discusses some of the stereotypes regarding nursing and highlights some of the inaccurate categorizations that often surround nursing, mostly because of media mischaracterizations. Students were asked to discuss this in their posting for the week, and this dialogue was one of the most animated discussions of the course. The discussion prompt asked the following:

> After viewing the video clip "I'm Just a Nurse" reflect on your impressions of it. What is the nurse's role? Are nurses "doctor's assistants"? Are nurses "just" nurses? What do you think about the stereotypes of nurses? How will you influence those stereotypical images of nursing? How would you manage a situation in which a client asked you to change the nurse assigned to them based on gender, race or ethnicity? Finally, what do you believe defines a nurse? and do you have a personal definition of nursing?

Students had an array of responses, and they were always remarkably respectful of one another's values and life situations. Here is an example:

> The decision to become a nurse was a somewhat difficult one for me because I was apprehensive as to what my family and friends would think, and if their reactions would be similar to how the people in the video clip responded in

regards to the role of nurses. To my dismay, my family thought I should try to be a doctor, and despite my protests, my mom is still intent on the idea of me becoming at least a physician's assistant.... what people fail to realize is the importance of nurses... they are the foundation, the frame, and the heartbeat of healthcare!... Whether helping to assess and monitor a patient's progress, or injecting intravenous medications and cleaning wounds, or even just listening to a patient, a nurse helps those he or she cares for in many different ways. It's a part of the job description, and male or female, a nurse should be a compassionate, caring, and comforting individual with the trained skill and knowledge to treat someone who is ill.

CONTENT AREAS: CULTURE

The content area that focuses on culture is particularly significant to nursing and is included in all nursing courses. To provide the best care possible, nurses must be able to assess and plan individualized care to clients from any culture. In this introductory nursing course, students are expected to develop a basic appreciation for why understanding and knowledge about multiple cultures is so critical in nursing. The face-to-face class offering presents students with a faculty-led discussion which asks students to consider what culture is, what ethnicity is, how to provide culturally-sensitive care, and what some of the stumbling blocks are in having effective cultural relationships. Students also complete a questionnaire concerning stereotypes and then view a film that provides insights into different ways of life in different cultures. The objective is for students to identify how culture impacts health and illness beliefs. Students then complete a homework assignment that asks them to review what they have watched, and to describe specifically how this film would help them provide individualized cross-cultural care. The first of the course's major assignments, the cultural assessment, is also due this week, as it requires students to investigate one individual's culture extensively. This is a brief assignment requiring students to interview someone from a culture other than their own, assessing their interviewees' culture, health beliefs and practices, values, and evaluating what factors would help a health care practitioner facilitate culture-specific health care for this individual.

Once again, there were some assignments that had to be altered slightly for the online course. Students were directed to complete the same readings, review the week's presentation handout, and to view the movie "*My Big Fat Greek Wedding.*" The homework assignment was developed to address both the readings and the film that students watched. For this assignment, students had to answer questions pertaining to one cultural group reviewed in their textbook. These questions ask students to reflect on the type of "healers" that other cultures use, in addition to beliefs about health, illness and society in general. For their discussion postings in this week, students were additionally asked to consider the following:

Health, illness, and caring have meanings that are unique to each culture. Please tell us a little bit about your culture and any special health/illness/ healing modality beliefs associated with your family or culture. Next, please tell us a little bit about any experiences you may have had with non-Western medicine? Have you ever been cared for or had contact with a cultural healer?

Students were very excited to share their family's cultural background and what some of their ethnic/cultural health and illness beliefs were. They were also very willing to share and teach the other students in the class about their experiences with non-Western medicine. Here is an example:

Growing up I played softball from the time I was five until my freshman year in college. I played . . . pitcher . . . my arm would get very sore . . . my neighbor is a doctor, and decided to try acupuncture to alleviate the pain in my arm. I was amazed at how my arm felt after a couple of treatments. IT WORKED!

For this content area students also completed the cultural assessment project. This project gave the students an opportunity to interview a potential client in a way that will enable them to gain understanding about the clients they may care for and to provide culturally-sensitive care. Students were given an interview guide that provides structure to their data collection by identifying the information that needs to be gathered. It asks for information about culture of origin, religion, family beliefs, health beliefs, and values/beliefs in general. Many students chose to interview friends or neighbors, and some even interviewed complete strangers—people they met while traveling during our online course. This assignment was done well by most of the students and was actually more diverse, in terms of age and culture, than is sometimes seen in the face-to-face class. Many of the students who participated in the first offering of this online course were traveling both nationally and internationally, and thus came into contact with a variety of cultures, something that students living on a small university campus during a regular semester would be less likely to do.

CONTENT AREAS: CRITICAL THINKING

Critical thinking is an essential component of nurses prepared with baccalaureate degrees. As an introduction to this expectation, students in this course learn to define the problem-solving process and its implications in professional nursing practice. The face-to-face course employs several critical thinking activities, including a game called "Murder Mystery." This game could not be adapted for the online course, as it asks students to break out into groups and they are each given a series of cards that enables them to solve a murder mystery. The ability to work together and to use basic problem-solving skills allows students to begin to see some of the elements involved in critical thinking, such as understanding, reasoning, reflection, judgment and creativity.

Alternate activities were developed for the online course. In addition to standard readings, students viewed three different video clips on critical thinking that were also part of the homework assignment questions. All three video clips were produced by The Foundation for Critical Thinking (www.criticalthinking.org) and present three parts of a lecture series by Dr. Richard Paul on the importance and components of critical thinking (The Foundation for Critical Thinking, 2008a, 2008b, 2008c). Finally, students were instructed on how to construct a concept map—a visual diagram showing the relationship among various concepts—that can be used in multiple disciplines. In nursing, concept maps are used as a way of synthesizing client problems and interventions that shows how they relate to one another (Potter & Perry, 2009). Students start completing a concept map pertaining to their paper topics to be completed later in the semester. As students completed this assignment the expectation was that they would begin to see how critical thinking activities such as concept mapping could help them synthesize information, both in this course and in their clinical nursing practice. An example of a student's concept map as it related to her paper topic on eating disorders can be found in Figure 10.3. Not every student's concept map was quite this well developed; however, most were very well done and allowed assessment of the students' ability to apply skills that promote critical thinking.

CONTENT AREAS: COMMUNICATION

Communication is one of the most in-depth topics, and traditionally stretches across two or more class periods. In this section students should be able to identify why effective communication is so essential for nurses, to differentiate therapeutic from non-therapeutic communication, and to begin to practice of therapeutic communication techniques. The face-to-face class on communication consists of lectures, usually over three different class periods, with a pause during the second class meeting to view three video vignettes demonstrating communication techniques. Following this viewing, there is a class discussion of whether the communication was done well or poorly and how it could be improved. After watching individual video clips students participate in classroom discussions about their observations about communication barriers or effective techniques. In the face-to-face

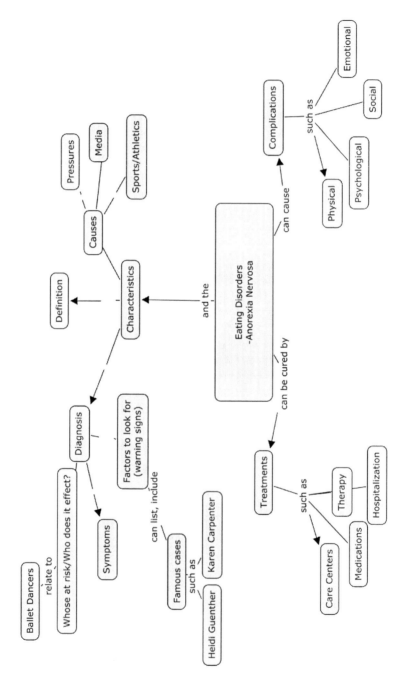

Figure 10.3 Sample Concept Map produced by students in the online version of NUR 103.

setting, students also analyze written case studies for therapeutic versus non-therapeutic communication between nurses and clients.

These vignettes were not available to for online viewing; thus an alternative had to be identified. This posed a dilemma in terms of the best teaching practices; however, after much thought and searching, I found a wonderful documentary video on Alzheimer's disease on the HBO web site. This documentary is based on a book by Maria Shriver and details the ways in which family members and other caregivers cope with the disease, as well as how they communicate with a loved on who has Alzheimer's. Students were then asked to respond to the following prompt:

> After viewing the documentary, "Grandpa, do you know who I am?" please reflect on your response to this film. Discuss whether or not you thought there was therapeutic or non-therapeutic communication being used and why or why not.

The film was poignant and the students were able to offer very pointed analytical observations regarding whether they believed therapeutic communication was achieved or not, and why. This documentary also offered students insight into how to make communication during illness more individual, and many of them shared personal stories from their own families.

This part of the course also includes an assignment called a "process recording," which is a written encounter of an interaction with a client. In a process recording, the health care provider writes down what the client communicated, both verbally and nonverbally, and what the nurse (or other health care provider) communicated, both verbally and nonverbally (Hames & Joseph, 1986). This assignment is used in the face-to-face course, and was easily adapted to the online version. This project gives the student an opportunity to participate in an interaction with a "client" (who can be a family member or friend, so long as it was a meaningful interaction), and then reflect on their own thoughts, feelings and perspectives—as well as the "client's" —during this interaction. The goal of the process recording is to allow students to assess how well they focus on client needs and, more importantly, how they can improve their communication style.

CONTENT AREAS: VALUES/ETHICS/LEGAL IMPLICATIONS

The unit regarding values, ethics and legal implications requires some presentation handouts, as there are quite a few definitions and ideas that may be somewhat unfamiliar to many students. This content area also calls for a fair amount of inward reflection as it relates to personal values and biases. The objective is that students begin to explore and identify ethical principles of professional nursing behavior. Students are introduced to some of the differences between ethical conduct and legal rights for both clients and nurses, and are expected to be able to identify the nurse's role in both. The traditional face-to-face class involves lectures, class discussion and group activities utilizing case studies.

The online course followed a similar format, with instructor-led discussion combined with viewing of a media clip produced by the Public Broadcast Service (PBS) regarding the ethics of healthcare rationing (Severson, 2008). After viewing this clip and completing the week's readings, students read a series of case studies concerning a client scenario involving either an ethical or legal dilemma, and then discussed how they would manage this situation as a healthcare professional. Students also had to answer homework questions and respond to online discussion questions pertaining to values/ethics and legal implications as they affect client care. The online prompts for this week included some of the following:

> Give an example of an ethical dilemma that you have encountered, experienced or heard about and discuss how you would/could process it using the 7 steps involved in processing an ethical dilemma. Also, after viewing the video clip "Ethics of Health Care Rationing," what do you think nurses' ethical or legal responsibilities are to undocumented clients?

The last question provoked the most discussion, especially because not all students agreed with one another. Some students were quite disturbed by the prospect of health care rationing, while others felt it was necessary for reduction in health care spending. No matter which position students took, they remained respectful of their classmates, yet offered insightful points on both sides of the issue.

CONTENT AREAS: HEALTH, WELLNESS AND ILLNESS

This section of the course is designed to help students gain an initial understanding of the concepts of health, wellness and illness. Students are introduced to a variety of different theoretical models that reflect health and wellness choices often made by individuals. The students are then introduced to some of the variations in chronic versus acute illness, the different levels of illness/disease prevention and treatment and, finally, what kind of variables impact illness and health behaviors. Students enrolled in the face-to-face version of this course complete readings, participate in class discussions and complete two questionnaires—developed specifically for this course—that involve self-reflection on individual health and wellness beliefs and practices.

These health and wellness questionnaires were incorporated into the online version as part of the students' homework assignment. Additionally, students viewed two internet video clips produced by a young woman living with postural orthostatic tachycardia syndrome (POTS) ("What is Postural Orthostatic Tachycardia Syndrome? Part one," 2008; "What is Postural Orthostatic Tachycardia Syndrome? Part Two," 2008). These two short films explore her daily routines and struggles, and how she is managing her illness. In the discussion prompt for this week students were asked to first explore their own personal definitions of health, wellness and illness, and then to reflect on the film clips. The students were amazed to see a young woman, not so different from themselves, coping with a very serious and life-altering chronic illness. They reflected on how well this young woman was still maintaining a relatively normal, yet very different lifestyle.

CONTENT AREAS: TEACHING AND LEARNING

Client and family teaching is a very large component of what nurses do; however, beginning nursing students usually do not expect as much emphasis to be placed on understanding of teaching and learning as there is. The intent in this course is that students will be able to discuss the professional helper's role as a teacher and demonstrate knowledge of teaching and group processes in the classroom. In the classroom, students are initially assigned to groups, and one student is then asked to explain to the group how to put on a jacket verbally, with no demonstration. A classroom conversation then follows, discussing the range of individual learning styles and needs, particularly health care consumers. This is followed by an instructor-led presentation that introduces various teaching concepts and how to include the nursing process in the teaching of clients. Students also complete a teaching and learning project pertaining to a health related topic and present it to the class.

The online conversion of this section was fairly simple and followed a similar format to others, with homework questions and discussion prompts. The format used for the teaching project in the face-to-face course was not an option for the students to present their projects, so an alternative had to be considered. Thus for the online class, the students were asked to choose a health-related topic that interested them and do some scholarly research on this topic (incorporating websites, articles, textbooks, etc.). They then had to develop a way of teaching this to the class—online. They were asked to approach this as if they were teaching a client who knows a limited amount of information about the topic. The students then had to link their teaching materials to a posting for the class to view. They were given presentations and pamphlets as examples of appropriate methods, but could choose other approaches as well. They were also asked to explain how they assessed the learner in terms of motivation and readiness to learn, how they planned to teach this subject, and how they would evaluate the effectiveness of their teaching. The students' projects allowed me to evaluate the students' ability to comprehend and demonstrate the importance of teaching and learning in nursing practice. The only aspect that I would alter for future offerings of this course would be to have the weekly posting for this unit revolve completely around the teaching project. The students put a great deal more effort into this than was anticipated, thus the discussion postings should focus on the teaching they aimed to do.

CONTENT AREAS: HEALTH CARE DELIVERY SYSTEMS

This unit was probably one of the most complex in terms of material. The face-to-face version includes an instructor presentation, followed by a film on who is at risk in the current health care crisis, and concludes with group work based on case studies on health care delivery systems. For the online class, first offered in the summer of 2009, there was no shortage of video clips regarding health care needs and health care reform—thanks to media coverage of President Obama's proposed national health care plan. Thus, after the students reviewed their readings and the presentation handout, they watched three clips on the most recent debates in U.S. health care delivery. The discussion posting and homework pertained to both the film clips and readings, which included questions concerning what students feel some of the greatest issues are in our current health care delivery system and what the role of nursing should be in helping the uninsured. Students were remarkably well-educated on the current state of affairs of health care reform and did a great job of synthesizing this with what they had learned in this course.

Students concluded the online course by writing a scholarly paper involving a more thorough investigation of a specific health care concept. This assignment provided students the opportunity to write a paper using scholarly documentation while comprehensively exploring one of the course concepts, as it related to a personal interest.

CHALLENGES AND OPPORTUNITIES

Professional Practice in Health and Illness introduces freshman students interested in nursing to the foundations of professional nursing. Nursing, in its purest essence, involves caring for those in need, either due to physical or mental illness. Thus, a large portion of nursing education takes place in the real world, caring for actual clients or in a simulated environment with "hands-on" learning. This made some of the course content challenging to convey in a faceless environment, and one of the most challenging tasks was to establish a sense of a professional relationship among the students, as well as with the course instructor.

One effective teaching strategy I used to establish a rapport between the students and me was for me to participate in the discussion postings. Many of the students commented that this meant a great deal to them, as they felt the instructor was "there" with them throughout the course. Also, discussions began with introductions, asking the students to tell the class who they were, and, more importantly, to tell the group why they were interested in nursing and what they thought nursing was. The last strategy used to build a sense of reality within this online environment was to include relevant media clips that enhanced the content they were learning about.

There were also several challenges that arose while I taught this course. One of the first things that manifested was how to manage "student issues," whether personal dilemmas or learning difficulties. For the most part these could be managed via private email discussions; however, there were a couple of times when speaking on the phone or meeting with a student in person was needed. As the summer session proceeded, it was easy to discern that the students were diverse in age, culture, and life experiences. Often the diversity was an extremely positive experience, as the slightly older students would actually write responses to some of the younger students in mentoring, yet thought-provoking ways. There were, however, a few times when students either shared inappropriate stories or used unsuitable language, and I replied privately to let them know that this was unacceptable.

Teaching this course was a learning experience for me, as online instruction challenges traditional teaching methods used in nursing education. However, teaching online also creates an environment that requires great focus on individual student work, thus a deeper understanding of each student often develops. It also allows for the wonderful opportunity to break out of the box and be very unconventional in the teaching of fundamental nursing knowledge, which can inspire exploration of different teaching techniques in other face-to-face courses! There is also a slight sense of greater impartiality in grading of assignments, probably because of the "facelessness" of the online environment. Even the most impartial educator may feel badly when giving a "nice" student a bad grade. Anonymity certainly aids in overcoming a sense of guilt and the sense of fear in trying something new!

REFERENCES

Field, T. (2002). Internet-based education for enrolled nurses: could it be e-ffective? *Australian Journal of Advanced Nursing, 19*(4), 33–37.

The Foundation for CriticalThinking (Producer). (2008a). Dr. Richard Paul On the Elements of Thought: Excerpts from the Socratic Questioning Series. *Critical Thinking and the Basic Elements of Thought* [Video podcast]. Retrieved from http://www.youtube.com/watch?v=_VPg_cGAfHk

The Foundation for CriticalThinking (Producer). (2008b). Dr. Richard Paul On the Intellectual Standards Part 2: Excerpts from the Socratic Questioning Series. *Critical Thinking—Standards of Thought—Part 2* [Video podcast]. Retrieved from http://www.youtube.com/watch?v=Ksk2-ayoBck&feature=related

The Foundation for CriticalThinking (Producer). (2008c) Dr. Richard Paul On the Intellectual Standards: Excerpts from the Socratic Questioning Series. *Critical Thinking—Standards of Thought—Part 1* [Video podcast]. Retrieved from http://www.youtube.com/watch?v=gNCOOUK-bMQ

G Raymond Chang School of Continuing Education, R. U. (Producer). (2008, May 25, 2009) I'm just a nurse [Video podcast]. Retrieved from http://www.youtube.com/watch?v=Jds1AlKzVGg

Hames, C., & Joseph, D. (Eds.). (1986). *Basic concepts of helping: A holistic approach* (2nd ed.). Norwalk, CT: Appleton-Century-Crofts.

Kenny, A. (2002). Online learning: enhancing nurse education? *Journal of Advanced Nursing, 38*(2), 127–135.

LaSala, K. B. & Nelson, J. (2005). What contributes to professionalism? *MedSurg Nurse, 14*(1), 63–67.

Lashley, M. (2005). Teaching health assessment in the virtual classroom. *Journal of Nuring Education, 44*(8), 348–350.

Potter, P., & Perry, A. (Eds.). (2009). *Fundamentals of Nursing* (7th ed.). St. Louis: Mosby.

Severson, L. (Producer). (2008). Ethics of Health Care Rationing. *Religion and Ethics* [Video podcast]. Retrieved from http://www.pbs.org/wnet/religionandethics/episodes/august-8-2008/ethics-of-health-care-rationing/16/

What is Postural Orthostatic Tachycardia Syndrom? Part One. (2008). Video podcast retrieved from http://www.youtube.com/watch?v=o5D9T04OVZg&feature=related

What is Postural Orthostatic Tachycardia Syndrome? Part Two. (2008). Video podcast retrieved from http://www.youtube.com/watch?v=vKrwFMnBvA4&feature=related

CONCLUSIONS

CHAPTER 11

AND IN CONCLUSION...

José A. Amador and Kathleen M. Torrens

Out of the wide variety of academic areas, course levels and experiences presented by the authors, a number of common threads arise from their experiences developing and teaching the classroom version of their courses online. Foremost among these is the need for *clarity*—in everything, from our syllabi to online communication. The syllabi for our classroom courses can serve as a starting point to establish this clarity in our online courses. Our contributors strive to achieve clarity in their online courses through construction of a syllabus that lays it all out *a priori* —everything from expectations for quality and frequency of communication, for content and structure of written assignments and postings, to deadlines for required work (and their consequences). The "rules of engagement" outlined in a syllabus can be further refined through the use of other devices that have proven effective in the classroom, such as rubrics. Rubrics in the online course continue to help us communicate our expectations clearly to students, whether they address the content and structure of discussion postings or provide feedback on papers.

Not only is clear communication key to the success of the online course; this communication needs to take place early and frequently. A common recommendation among our contributors is that you contact students in advance—weeks in advance, in many cases—with information about your-

Taking Your Course Online: An Interdisciplinary Journey, pages 133–135
Copyright © 2012 by Information Age Publishing
All rights of reproduction in any form reserved.

self, your course, and your syllabus. This early interaction helps set the tone for your course. It is also critical that communication be frequent—to allay fears, clarify (there's that word again) ambiguous statements, to provide feedback and/or direct online discussions, to explain where a student went wrong (or right) in her homework. Frequent communication can head off small misunderstandings before they become unmanageable problems.

The need for self-discipline in both students and instructors also comes across in most chapters. The apparent absence of temporal structure in on-line courses can be a deceptive lure to students that choose to take courses online, particularly during the summer. The expectations of a leisurely, self-paced class are met with the harsh reality of having to "make time" for what was otherwise imposed from outside in the classroom setting. In addition, the absence of the physical rituals associated with "going to class" can make online courses an even greater challenge for students. The successful on-line student thus needs sufficient intellectual and emotional maturity to take responsibility for his class participation. Whether they state this ex-plicitly or implicitly, the authors have helped students with the transition from the classroom by implementing a temporal structure in their online courses—through activities such as recurring posting of prompts and as-sociated online discussions, deadlines for homework and papers, and set dates and times for tests. Furthermore, effective prompts, questions and problems can help the "Discussion" board or forum to take the place of the classroom as the space for interaction among students and instructors.

One clear advantage of the transformation from the classroom to online is an improvement in the quality and quantity of student written commu-nication. Whether they teach landscape architecture or soil science, our authors generally found that students' ability to communicate in writing online was an improvement over face-to-face oral communication in the classroom, particularly in the context of class discussions. This often-un-anticipated benefit of the online class environment is likely the result of students having more time: to understand what's being asked, to focus on the important issues, and to articulate their responses. The corollary to improved written communication in online courses is that this learning en-vironment puts those students with low writing and reading skills at a dis-advantage, as is pointed out in a number of chapters. In the highly textual medium that is the web, students that with good literacy skills will have a leg up on those that do not.

In addition to the many common themes threaded through these chap-ters, there are a number of unique insights into the process of converting your course to online. For example, Reyes, Martin and Costello speak to the difficulties presented by trying to translate successful classroom discussions to the online environment. Problems such as limited enrollment in online courses can put a crimp on these discussions, with the lack of critical mass limiting the range of ideas and the amount of course material addressed as part of these discussions. Differences in levels of literacy among students can exacerbate these difficulties online relative to the classroom.

Along the same lines, Misto points out that not all classroom activities can be re-engineered for easy translation into online. Trying to turn the "Squares" game—a successful team-building activity in her face-to-face introductory nursing course—into an online activity turned out not to be practical. Rather than give up, she describes re-thinking the activity to accomplish same goal as the game: to get nursing students to think about what is required for effective teamwork. Although the "icebreaker" aspect of it was lost, the use of movies and discussion prompts proved effective in getting students to ponder the basics of teamwork.

Immediacy—the rapport we develop with our students in face-to-face classes—is an important motivation for student learning, and one would perhaps expect this to be one of the early casualties of taking a course online. However, as DiCioccio points out, this need not be so. By concentrating on the use of verbal immediacy techniques in the online version of her family communication course, she strives to accomplish the same level of immediacy experiences in the classroom. Those that she has found successful include revealing appropriate personal information, personalizing feedback and publicly praising outstanding work.

Getting students to work successfully in groups can be a challenge in our face-to-face courses, although one that is often worth the effort on our part because the opportunities for our students to learn are enhanced greatly by group interactions. Translating successful group activities to the online environment can, however, prove very difficult. Thus Martin's very successful collaborative final project in her Writing Health and Disability course—a policy piece with recommendations for meeting ADA requirements on campus—did not survive the transition to online because of logistic limitations. By contrast, Amador found that the groups in his online Problem-Based Learning soil science course worked more effectively than in the classroom version of the course; discussions among group members were more focused and extensive, and the content and quality of the written work they produced was better.

Whether you are working on changing your bricks-and-mortar course to online for the first time, fine-tuning an existing course taught in cyberspace, or merely contemplating the idea of doing so, we hope that the experiences we describe here have been of use. We have presented the good, the bad and the ugly in the spirit of helping fellow faculty who are on the road to online pedagogy. We hope you have gotten as much out of reading this book as we have writing it.

ABOUT THE AUTHORS

Kathleen Torrens has taught several courses online over the past eight years. Formerly a confirmed skeptic of the pedagogical efficacy of online teaching and learning, she has published, solely and with co-authors, scholarly articles on the subject, with a focus on pedagogy and best practices. An associate professor, she teaches courses—face-to-face as well as online—in rhetoric, public address and women's studies for the departments of Communication Studies and Women's Studies at the University of Rhode Island, where she has taught for eight years.

José Amador is a professor in the Department of Natural Resources Science at the University of Rhode Island. He has a B.S. in biochemistry, and M.S. and Ph.D. in Soil Science, all from Cornell University. José has been on the faculty at the University of Rhode Island for the past 19 years, where he has taught Introduction to Soil Science to more than 1,200 students using lecture and problem-based learning formats. He is the author—with Libby Miles and C.B. Peters—of *The Practice of Problem-Based Learning: A Guide to Implementing PBL in the College Classroom* (Anker, 2007). He has led workshops and published on the use of problem-based learning in the college classroom.

Taking Your Course Online: An Interdisciplinary Journey, pages 137–138
Copyright © 2012 by Information Age Publishing
All rights of reproduction in any form reserved.

CONTRIBUTOR LIST

All at the University of Rhode Island, Kingston, Rhode Island

José A. Amador, Ph.D., Professor, Department of Natural Resources Science

Farhad Atash, Ph.D., Professor, Program in Landscape Architecture

James Baglama, Ph.D., Associate Professor, Department of Mathematics

Barbara Costello, Ph.D., Associate Professor, Department of Sociology and Anthropology

Rachel L. DiCioccio, Ph.D., Associate Professor, Department of Communication Studies

Celest Martin, Ph.D., Associate Professor, Program in Writing and Rhetoric

Kara Misto, M.S., R.N., Instructor, College of Nursing

Ian Reyes, Ph.D., Assistant Professor, Department of Communication Studies

Adam David Roth, Ph.D., Assistant Professor, Department of Communication Studies

Kathleen M. Torrens, Ph.D., Associate Professor, Department of Communication Studies

CPSIA information can be obtained at www.ICGtesting.com
Printed in the USA
LVOW070957101012

302261LV00001B/115/P